GLEANINGS FROM THE PAST
EXTRACTS FROM THE WRITINGS OF WILLIAM GURNALL

Gleanings from William Gurnall

selected by
Hamilton Smith

Soli Deo Gloria Publications
...for instruction in righteousness...

Soli Deo Gloria Publications
P.O. Box 451, Morgan, PA 15064
(412) 221-1901/FAX 221-1902

*

Gleanings from William Gurnall was first published as *Gleanings from the Past: Extracts from the Writings of William Gurnall* by the Central Bible Truth Depot in London in 1914. This Soli Deo Gloria reprint is 1996.

*

ISBN 1-57358-010-4

PREFACE

THE extracts that form this little volume are gleaned from a well-known Puritan work, written by William Gurnall and published in 1665, entitled, "The Christian in Complete Armour."

Amongst all the Puritan writings that have come down to us, none, perhaps, are more practical and conscience-reaching than this notable work. The perusal of the following pages will prove it still to be a ministry, rich with glowing thoughts to warm the heart;— a quiver well stocked with arrows to reach the conscience.

H. S.

1914.

CONTENTS

		PAGE
PREFACE	. . . . .	v
BIOGRAPHICAL INTRODUCTION	.	ix

CHAPTER		
I.	SIN AND GUILT	1
II.	PROFESSION AND HYPOCRISY .	11
III.	PRIDE AND WORLDLINESS . .	23
IV.	GLAD TIDINGS AND JOY . .	32
V.	FAITH AND HOLINESS . . .	45
VI.	WILES AND TEMPTATIONS . .	54
VII.	SUFFERING AND SHAME . . .	64
VIII.	STRIFE AND CONTENTION . .	78
IX.	SERVANTS AND SERVICE . . .	90
X.	READING AND MEDITATION . .	100
XI.	PRAYER AND THANKSGIVING . .	109
XII.	PATIENCE AND HOPE . . .	129
XIII.	A BASKET OF FRAGMENTS . .	138

BIOGRAPHICAL INTRODUCTION

OF the personal history of William Gurnall hardly anything is known. Such bald facts as we possess are mainly gathered from a somewhat rare book, printed in 1830, and compiled by a painstaking antiquarian, named M'Keon. It is entitled, " An Inquiry into the Birthplace, Parentage, Life, and Writings of the Rev. William Gurnall, formerly Rector of Lavenham, in Suffolk, and author of 'The Christian in Complete Armour.'"

From this dry-as-dust little volume we learn that Gurnall was born at the seaport of Lynn, in the county of Norfolk, in the year 1616. He received his early education at the Free Grammar School of that town, passing, in 1632, to Emmanuel College, Cambridge. He graduated B.A. in 1635, and M.A. in 1639. No record remains to tell us how he spent the next five years of his life, with the exception of a passing remark, in one of Gurnall's letters, which would

x BIOGRAPHICAL INTRODUCTION

suggest that he was preaching at Sudbury for some portion of the time.

In December, 1644, he was appointed Minister of the Parish of Lavenham in Suffolk. Here he spent the remainder of his life exercising his ministry for a period of thirty-five years. The year following this appointment, Gurnall was married to Sarah Mott, daughter of the Rev. Thomas Mott. By this lady he had ten children, eight of whom survived him.

Gurnall died October the 12th, 1679, in his sixty-third year, and was buried at Lavenham. The exact spot of his burial is unknown, no stone or monument recording the resting-place of his body.

Such is the bare outline of his history; but one other fact, that has given rise to much difference of judgment, remains to be noticed. In 1662, on the passing of the Act of Uniformity, when some two thousand ministers were ejected from the Church of England, Gurnall conformed to the Act, signed the required declaration, and retained his position as Rector of Lavenham.

That a preacher of such decided Puritan views should retain his connection with the Church of England at a time when, on every hand, godly and devoted men were seceding for conscience sake, seems inexplicable. There still exists a printed attack on Gurnall published in 1665, which, scurrilous as it is, yet clearly indicates that his action received strong condemnation at the time, and exposed him to severe reproach. This attack takes the form of two letters written to Gurnall by an anonymous author who calls himself a "Christian Friend." The title of this remarkable production is "Covenant Renouncers, Desperate Apostates," and the public are informed that it is "Printed in Anti-turn-coat Street, and sold at the Sign of Truth's Delight, right opposite to Backsliding Alley." The contents of the pamphlet are quite in keeping with the title-page, and hence it will be readily understood there is nothing very 'Christian,' or 'friendly,' in the letters of this "Christian Friend."

We may hold different opinions as to Gurnall's action, we may form conjectures as to the motives that prompted him in his decision, but no scrap of evidence remains to enlighten us as to the private views or personal motives that actuated him in conforming to the Act. To his own Master he must stand or fall.

From his funeral sermon, preached by William Burkitt, we may gather that Gurnall suffered from a weakly body which often kept him confined to his house. Burkitt describes him as a man of great humility, a man who loved the Lord, loved souls, and loved the saints, and one, too, who deplored the bitter religious controversies that raged among the Christian professors of his day. The words of Burkitt are worth quoting : " How often did he publicly deplore and bewail, that the greatest measure of love that is found at this day amongst the professors of the cross, was not true Christian love, *but only love of a party.*" Burkitt winds up his discourse by describing him as a CHRISTIAN IN COMPLETE ARMOUR.

H. S.

Gleanings from the Past

I

SIN AND GUILT

"The way of transgressors is hard."
PROVERBS xiii. 15.

THE terror of sin. A soul in a state of sin may possess much, but enjoys nothing. One thought of its state of enmity to God, would drop bitterness into every cup; all he hath smells of hell-fire; and a man at a rich feast would enjoy it but little if he smelt fire, ready to burn his house and himself.

The love of sin. Sin is as truly the offspring of the soul, as children are of our bodies, and it finds as much favour in our eyes, yea, more; for the sinner can slay a son to save a sin alive (Micah vi. 7).

The pleasures of sin. The pleasures of sin must needs be short, because life cannot be long, and they both end together. Indeed, many times the pleasure of sin dies before the man dies: sinners live to bury their joy in this world. The worm breeds in their conscience before it breeds in their flesh by death. But be sure the pleasure of sin never survives this world. The word is gone out of God's mouth, every sinner "shall lie down in sorrow" and wake in sorrow. . . . The carnal heart is all for the present; his snout is in the trough, and while his draught lasts, he thinks it will never end. Who would envy the condemned man his feast which he hath in his way to the gallows?

Where guilt is contracted in the getting of an enjoyment, there can be little sweetness tasted when it comes to be used. There is a great difference between the joy of the husbandman, at the getting in of his corn at the harvest, and the thief's joy, who hath stolen some sheaves out of another's field, and is making merry with his booty.

SIN AND GUILT

No sin goes single. It is impossible to embrace or allow one sin, and be free of others. Allow one sin, and God will give you over to others. When Judas began to play the thief, I question whether he meant to turn traitor; no, his treason was a punishment for his thievery.

Secret sins. God is privy to thy most secret sin, "Thou hast set our iniquities before Thee, our secret sins in the light of Thy countenance" (Psa. xc. 8). As He sees when thou shuttest thy closet to pray, and will reward thy sincerity: so when thou dost it to sin in secret, He will reward thy hypocrisy. The word tells thee of an informer which thou hast in thy own bosom,—conscience, which goes along with thee, and is witness to all thy fine-laid plots, and what it sees it writes down, for it is a court of record. Thou canst not sin so fast but it can write after thee; and the pen with which conscience writes down our sins hath a sharp point, it cuts deep into the very heart and soul of the sinner.... Consult the word, and thou wilt find that

God usually hath put them to shame in this world, who have promised themselves most secrecy in their sinning. So Gehazi played his part cunningly enough, which made him so bold to come before his master, and impudently lie to his head, not dreaming the least that he was aware of his sin; yet this man is found out, and for the garments he got of Naaman by a lie, he had another given of the Lord, which he was to wear as a livery for his sin, for he was clothed with a leprosy: a garment more lasting than the two changes of suits he had from the Syrian; for this lasted him all his life; neither was it then worn out, but to be put on by his children after him (2 Kings v. 27). Yea, be he a saint, yet if he goes about to save himself from the shame of a sin, by any secret plot of wickedness, he takes the direct way to bring that upon him which he contrives to keep off. Uriah's blood was shed only as a sinful expedient to save David's credit. Ah, poor man! all comes out to his greater shame. David shall know that God will be as tender of His own honour, as he is of his credit;

SIN AND GUILT

"For thou didst it secretly: but I will do this thing before all Israel, and before the sun" (2 Sam. xii. 12).

Bosom sins. Satan labours to provoke the Christian to heart sins, to stir up and foment these inward motions of sins in the Christian's bosom; he knows his credit now is not so great with the soul as when it was his slave; he must not think to command another's servant as his own; no, all he can do, is to watch the fittest season, when the Christian least suspects, and then to present some sinful motion handsomely dressed up to the eye of the soul, that the Christian may, before he is aware, take this brat up, and handle it in his thoughts, till at last he makes it his own by embracing it; and may be, this boy, sent in at the window, may open the door to let in a greater thief.

There may be more wickedness in a sin of the heart than of the hand. The more of the heart and spirit is let out, the more malignity is let in to any sinful act. To backslide in heart, is more than to backslide; it is the comfort of a poor soul when tempted and troubled for his relapses, that though his foot slides back, yet his heart turns not back, but faceth heaven and Christ at the same time; so to err in the heart, is worse than to have an error in the head; therefore God aggravates Israel's sin with this, "They do always err in their heart" (Heb. iii. 10). Their hearts run them upon the error; they liked idolatry, and so were soon made to believe what pleased them best. Peter lays the accent of Magus's sin on the wicked thought, which his words betrayed to be in his heart: "Pray God, if perhaps the thought of thine heart may be forgiven" (Acts viii. 22).

Say not thou lovest Christ, so long as thou canst lay those sins in thy bosom, which plucked His heart out of His bosom. It were strange if a child should keep, and delight to use, no other knife but that wherewith his father was stabbed.

SIN AND GUILT 7

Deliberate sins. Take heed of deliberate sin; like a stone thrown into a clear stream, it will so disturb thy soul, and muddy it, that thou, who even now could see thy interest in Christ, wilt now be at a loss, and know not what to think of thyself. Like a fire on the top of the house, it will be no easy matter to quench it. If thou hast been so unhappy as to fall into such a slough, take heed of lying in it by impenitence: the sheep may fall into a ditch, but it is the swine that wallows in it.

Presumptuous sins. Presumptuous sins are the thieves that break through and steal the saint's comfort away. When the Christian comes to look into his soul after such a bold act, and thinks to entertain himself, as formerly, with the comforts of his pardoned state, interest in Christ, and hopes of heaven through Him, alas! he finds a sad change; no promise that will give out its consolations to him. The cellar door is locked, Christ withdrawn, and the keys carried away with Him. Hast thou fallen into the hands of any such presumptuous sins; that have stolen thy peace from thee? Send speedily thy hue and cry after them. I mean, make thy sad moan to God, renew thy repentance out of hand, and raise heaven upon them by a spirit of prayer. This is no time to delay; the further thou lettest these sins go without repentance, the harder thou wilt find it to recover thy lost peace and joy out of their hands.

As presumptuous sins are the thieves, that with a high hand rob the Christian of his comfort; so sloth and negligence are as the rust, that in time will fret into his comfort, and eat out the heart and strength of it.

A thorn in the foot will make any way uneasy to the traveller, and guilt in the conscience any condition uncomfortable to the Christian, but most of all a suffering one. O it is sad, to go with sore and smarting consciences into a suffering condition.

Forsaking sin. "Let the wicked forsake

his way, and the unrighteous man his thoughts: and let him return unto the Lord, and He will have mercy upon him; and to our God, for He will abundantly pardon" (Isa. lv. 7). Some men's sins forsake them; "the unclean spirit goes out," and is not driven out; occasions to sin cease, or bodily ability to execute the commands of sin is wanting. To forsake sin, is to leave it without any thought reserved of returning to it again. It were strange to find a drunkard so constant in the exercise of that sin but some time you may find him sober; and yet a drunkard he is, as well as if he was then drunk. Every one hath not forsaken his trade, that we see now and then in their holiday suit; then the man forsakes his sin, when he throws it from him, and bolts the door upon it, with a purpose never to open more to it: "Ephraim shall say, What have I to do any more with idols?" (Hosea xiv. 8).... Forsake all or none; save one lust, and you lose your soul. What wilt thou get, poor sinner, if thou goest to hell, though thou goest thither by thy ignorance, unbelief, or spiritual pride, yet escape the plague of open profaneness? This is as ridiculous as it was with him, who being to be hanged, desired that he might by no means go through such a street to the gallows, for fear of the plague that was there.

Soul, take thy lust, thy only lust, which is the child of thy dearest love, thy Isaac, the sin which has caused most joy and laughter, from which thou hast promised thyself the greatest return of pleasure or profit, and offer it up; run the sacrificing knife of mortification into the very heart of it, and all this now, before thou hast one embrace more from it.

II

PROFESSION AND HYPOCRISY

"The hypocrite's hope shall perish."—JOB viii. 13.

SUCH a generation there ever was and shall be, that mingle themselves with the saints of God; who pretend heaven, with heavenly speeches, while their hearts are lined with hypocrisy, whereby they deceive others, and most of all themselves; such may be the world's saints, but devil's in Christ's account. "Have not I chosen you twelve, and one of you is a devil?" And truly, of all devils, none so bad as the professing devil, the preaching, praying devil.

Satan can live very peaceably, as a quiet neighbour, by the door of such as will content themselves with an empty name of profession; this alters not his property. Judas's profession, he knew, did not put him a step out of his way to hell; the devil can show a man a way to damnation through duties and ordinances of God's worship. That covetous, traitorous heart which Judas carried with him to hear Christ's sermon, and preach his own, held him fast enough to the devil; and therefore he gives him line enough, liberty enough to keep his credit a while with his fellow apostles; he cares not though others think him a disciple of Christ, so he knows him to be his own slave.

The hypocrite at first blush may be taken for a saint, by such as see only his outside, as he passeth by in his holiday dress, and therefore is fitly by one called the stranger's saint, but a devil to those who know him better.

The hypocrite can show a clear tongue, and yet have a foul heart; he that made that proverb, *Loquere ut te videam*, "Speak that I may see you," did not think of the hypocrite, who will speak that you shall not see him.

PROFESSION AND HYPOCRISY 13

He that hath a false end in his profession will soon come to the end of his profession, when he is pinched on that toe where his corn is; I mean, called to deny that his naughty heart aimed at.

Many there are that have nothing to prove themselves Christians but a naked profession, of whom we may say as they do of the cinnamon tree, that the bark is more worth than all they have besides.

==Many take up their saintship upon trust, and trade in religion with the credit they have gained from others' opinion of them. They believe themselves to be Christians, because others hope them to be such; and so their great business is, by a zeal in those exercises of religion that lie outermost, to keep up the credit they have abroad, but do not look to get a stock of solid grace within; and this proves their undoing at last. They say trees shoot as much in the root underground as in the branches above, and so doth true grace. Remember what was the==

perishing of the seed in stony ground! it lacked root; and why so but because it was stony? Be willing the plough should go deep enough to humble thee *for* sin, and rend thy heart *from* sin.

A hypocrite never got pardon in the disguise of a saint. He will call thee by thy own name, though thou comest to Him in the semblance of a penitent: "Come in, thou wife of Jeroboam," said the prophet. Hypocrisy is too thin a veil to blind the eyes of the Almighty. Thou mayest put thy own eyes out, so as not to see Him, but thou canst never blind His eyes so that He should not see thee.

Speak, O ye hypocrites! can you show one tear that ever you shed in earnest for a wrong done to God? It is a good gloss Augustine hath upon Esau's tears (Heb. xii.): "He wept that he lost the blessing, not that he sold it."

Time-serving. The hypocrite sets his

PROFESSION AND HYPOCRISY 15

watch, not by the sun, the Word I mean, but by the town clock; what most do, that he will do; *vox populi* is his *vox Dei*.

Self-righteousness. Take heed uprightness proves not a snare to thee. The young man in the gospel might have been better, had he not been so good. His honesty and moral uprightness was his undoing, or rather his conceit of them. Better he had been a publican, driven to Christ in the sense of his sin, than a Pharisee, kept from Him with an opinion of his integrity. May be thou art honest and upright in thy course. Bless God for it, but take heed of blessing thyself in it: there is the danger; this is one way of being "righteous over much." There is undoing in this over-doing, as well as in any under-doing.

What men do *by* themselves, they do *for* themselves; they devour the praise of what they do. The Christian only that doth all *by* Christ, doth all *for* Christ. Many souls do not only perish, praying, repenting, and believing after a sort, but they perish by their praying and repenting, while they carnally trust in these.

Few so bad indeed but seem to like religion in the *notion;* but *living* and *walking* holiness bites; the pharisees can lavish out their money on the prophets' tombs; but Christ is scorned and hated. What is the mystery of this? The reason was, these prophets are off the stage and Christ is on.

False zeal. Zeal without uprightness is of no service, nay, no one will go to hell with more shame than the false-hearted zealot, who mounts up towards heaven in his fiery chariot. Be not loth to be searched; there will need then no further search to prove thee unsound; if God's officers be denied entrance, all is not right within. If thy heart is sincere, it will delight in privacy. A false heart calls others to witness his zeal for God. It is the trick of the hypocrite to strain himself to the utmost in duty when he hath spectators, and to be careless alone.

A false heart may seem very hot in praying against one sin, but can skip over another; a hypocrite will be favourable to one lust, and violent against another; whereas a sincere Christian abhors all sin: " Order my steps in thy word: and let not *any* iniquity have dominion over me " (Psa. cxix. 133).

The hypocrite seems hot *in prayer*, but you will find him cold enough *at work*; he prays very fiercely against his sins, as if he desired them to be all slain upon the place; but doth he set himself upon the work of mortification? Doth he withdraw the fuel that feeds them?

Hypocrisy in religion springs from the bitter fruit of some carnal affection unmortified. So long as thy prey lie below, thy eye will be on the earth, when thou seemest, like an eagle, to mount in thy prayers to heaven. God is in the hypocrite's mouth, but the world is in his heart, which he expects to gain through his good reputation. . . . No man can say that Jesus is the Lord, but by the Holy Ghost (1 Cor. xii. 3). A man may say the words, without any special work of the Spirit, and so may a parrot : but to say Christ is Lord believingly, with thoughts and affections comporting with the greatness and sweetness thereof, requires the Spirit of God to be in his heart.

Knowledge without grace. An orthodox judgment with an unholy heart and ungodly life is as uncomely as a man's head would be on a beast's shoulders. That man hath little cause to boast that what he *holds* is truth, if what he *doth* be wicked.

Knowledge may make thee a scholar, but not a saint ; orthodox, but not gracious. He that increaseth in knowledge, and doth not get grace with his knowledge, increaseth sorrow to himself, yea, eternal sorrow. It would be an ease to gospel sinners in hell, if they could erase the remembrance of the gospel out of their memories.

He that can venture on the appearance of evil under pretence of liberty, may, for ought I know, commit that which is more grossly evil, under some appearance of good; it is not hard, if a man will be at the cost, to put a good colour on rotten stuff and practice also. . . . It is possible a man may have a rotten body under a gaudy suit; and under fine language, a poor ragged conscience. Who had not rather be sincere with mean gifts, than rotten-hearted with great parts?

Hypocrisy exposed. The Christian, like a star in the heavens, wades through the cloud, that for a time hides his comfort; but the hypocrite, like a meteor in the air, blazeth a little, and then drops into some ditch or other, where it is quenched. "The light of the righteous rejoiceth: but the lamp of the wicked shall be put out" (Prov. xiii. 9.).

Sincerity enables the Christian to do two things in affliction which the hypocrite cannot—to speak good *of* God, and to expect good *from* God.

"Will he always call upon God?" (Job xxvii. 10). The hypocrite is often exposed here. An unsound heart will be meddling with prayer now and then, but grows weary of the work at last, especially if he be made to wait long for an answer. Saul prays to God, and because he hears not from Him, goes at last to seek the devil.

One spot occasions the whole garment to be washed. David overcome with one sin, renews his repentance for all (Psa. li.). A good husband, when he seeth it raining at one place, sends for the workmen to look over all the house. This indeed, differenceth a sincere heart from an hypocrite, whose repentance is partial, soft in one plot and hard in another. Judas cries out of his treason, but not a word of his thievery and hypocrisy. The hole was no wider in his conscience than where the bullet went in; whereas true sorrow for one, breaks the heart into shivers for others also.

If profession would serve the turn, and

PROFESSION AND HYPOCRISY 21

flocking after sermons with some seeming joy at the word were enough to save, heaven would soon be full: but as you love your souls, do not try yourselves by this coarse sieve; that is, seek by an easy profession, and cheap religion, such as is hearing the word, performance of duties and the like; of this kind there are many that will come and walk about heaven's door, willing enough to enter, if they may do it without ruffling their pride in a crowd, or hazarding their present carnal interest by any contest and scuffle. Take Christians under the notion of "seekers," and, by Christ's own words, there are many; but consider them under the notion of "strivers," such as stand ready shod with a holy resolution, to strive even to blood, if such trails meet them in the way to heaven, rather than not enter, and then the number of Christian soldiers will shrink, like Gideon's goodly host, to a little troop.

In this old age of England's withered profession, how great a rarity is a sincere convert! When we see a tree that used to stand thick with fruit, now bring forth but little, maybe an apple on this bough, and another on that, we look upon it as a dying tree. Those golden days of the gospel are over, when converts came flying as a cloud, as the doves to the window in flocks. Now gospel news grows stale, few are taken with it. Our old store of saints, the treasure of their times, wears away apace; what will become of us, if no new ones come in their room? Alas! when our burials are more than our births, we must needs be on the losing hand. There is a sad list of holy names taken away from us; but where are they which are born to God? If the good go, and those which are left continue bad, yea, become worse and worse, we have reason to fear that God is clearing the ground, and making way for a judgment.

None sink so far into hell as those that come nearest heaven, because they fall from the greatest height. None will have such a sad parting from Christ as those who went half way with Him, and then left Him.

III

PRIDE AND WORLDLINESS

"A man's pride shall bring him low."
                    Proverbs xxix. 23.

*R*ELIGIOUS *Pride.* Some are blind as Laodicea, and know it not (Rev. iii. 17). As ignorance blinds the mind, so pride is a blind before their ignorance, that they know it not. These have such a high opinion of themselves that they take it ill that any should suspect them as such; these of all men are most out of the way to knowledge; they are too good to learn of man, as they think, and too bad to be taught of God. The gate into Christ's school is low, and these cannot stoop: the Master Himself is so humble and lowly that He will not teach a proud scholar.

Ah, poor creatures, what a sad change have they made, to leave the word, which can no more deceive them than God Himself to trust the guidance of themselves to themselves. "He that is his own teacher," saith Bernard, "is sure to have a fool for a master."

[margin note: NOT ALWAYS!]

Never art thou less holy than when puffed up with the conceit of it. "Behold, his soul which is lifted up is not upright" (Hab. ii. 4). See an *ecce*, like a sign, is set up at the proud man's door, that all passengers may know that a wicked man dwells there.

When men stand high their heads do not grow dizzy till they look down; when men look down upon those that are worse than themselves, or less holy than themselves, then their heads turn round; looking up would cure this disease. The most holy men, when once they have fixed their eyes awhile upon God's holiness, and then looked upon themselves, have been quite out of love with themselves. After the vision the prophet had of God sitting upon the throne, and the seraphim about Him, covering their faces,

PRIDE AND WORLDLINESS 25

and crying, "Holy, holy, holy, is the Lord of hosts," how was this gracious man smitten with the sense of his own vileness! they did no more cry up God as holy than he did cry out upon himself as unclean (Isa. vi. 5). So Job, "Now mine eye seeth Thee. Wherefore I abhor myself" (Job xlii. 5, 6).

Compare not thyself with those that have less than thyself, but look on those that have far exceeded thee: to look on our inferiors occasions pride. "I am not as this publican," saith the Pharisee; but looking on others more eminent than ourselves will both preserve humility, and be a spur to diligence.

A man may be very zealous in prayer and painstaking in preaching, and all the while pride is the master whom he serves, though in God's livery. It is hard starving this sin; there is nothing almost but it can live on; nothing so base that a proud heart will not be lifted up with, and nothing so sacred but it will profane. . . . So far as pride prevails the man prays and preaches rather to be thought good by others, rather to enthrone himself than Christ, in the opinion and hearts of his hearers.

Remember, Christian, when thou hast thy best suit on, who made it, who paid for it: thy grace, thy comfort, is neither the work of thy own hands, nor the price of thy own desert; be not for shame proud of another's cost. [*What do you have that you have not received?*]

Pride of gifts. If once (like Hezekiah) we call in spectators to see our treasure and applaud us for our gifts and comfort, then it is high time for God to send some messengers to carry these away from us, which carry our hearts from Him. . . . Pride of gifts hinders the receiving of good from others. Pride fills the soul, and a full soul will take nothing from God, much less from man.

Joseph's coat made him finer than his brethren, but caused all his trouble; thus great gifts lift a saint up a little higher in the eyes of men, but it occasions many

PRIDE AND WORLDLINESS

temptations which thou meetest not with that are kept low; what with envy from their brethren, malice from Satan, and pride in their own hearts, I dare say none find so hard a work to bear up against those waves and winds.

While thou art priding in thy gifts, thou art dwindling and withering in thy grace. Such are like corn that runs up much into straw, whose ear commonly is light and thin. Grace is too much neglected where gifts are too highly prized ; we are commanded to be clothed with humility. . . . Pride kills the spirit of praise : when thou should bless God, thou art applauding thyself. It destroys Christian love, and stabs our fellowship with the saints to the heart : a proud man hath not room enough to walk in company, because the gifts of others he thinks stand in his way. Pride so distempers the palate that it can relish nothing that is drawn from another's vessel. . . . Pride loves to climb up, not as Zaccheus, to see Christ, but to be seen himself,

"God resisteth the proud" (James iv. 6). The humble man may have Satan at his right hand to oppose him; but be sure the proud man shall find God Himself there to resist him. We must either lay self aside or God will lay us aside. . . . A proud scholar and a humble master will never agree: Christ is humble and lowly, and so resists the proud, but giveth grace to the humble.

Love of the world. Tell some of adding faith to faith, one degree of grace to another, and you shall find they have more mind to join house to house, and lay field to field; their souls are athirst, but not for Christ or heaven: it is earth, earth, they never think they have enough of, till death comes and stops their mouth with a shovelful digged out of their own grave!

The canker and rust of our gold and silver, which is got with harder labour than is required here, will rise up in judgment against many, and say, "You could drudge and trudge for us that are now turned to rust and dust, but could walk over the field of the word, where an incorruptible treasure lay, and would lose it rather than your sloth!"

Thy time is short and thy way long. Is it wisdom to lay out so much on thy tenement which thou art leaving, and forget what thou must carry with thee? Before the fruit of these be ripe which thou art now planting, thyself may be rotting in the grave: "Time is short," saith the apostle (1 Cor. vii. 29).

Men are very kind to themselves: first they wish it may be long before death comes; and then because they would have it so, they are bold to promise themselves it shall be so. Who makes the lease? the tenant or the landlord? . . . Thou art young, thou canst not therefore say, thou shalt not die as yet: alas! measure the coffins in the churchyard, and thou wilt find some of thy length: young and old are within the reach of death's scythe; old men, indeed, go to death, their age calls for it; but young men cannot hinder death's coming to them.

It is an ill time to caulk the ship when at sea, tumbling up and down in a storm : this should have been looked to when on her seat in the harbour. And as bad it is to begin to trim a soul for heaven, when tossing on a sick-bed. Things that are done in a hurry are seldom done well. These poor creatures, I am afraid, go in an ill dress to another world who begin to provide for it when on a dying bed. . . . There is but one heaven : miss that, and where can you take up your lodging but in hell ? One Christ that can lead you thither : reject Him, " and there remains no more sacrifice for sin."

O, how many part with Christ at the crossway ! like Orpah, that go a furlong or two with Christ, until He goes to take them off from their worldly hopes, and bids them prepare for hardship, and then they fairly kiss and leave Him ; loath indeed to lose heaven, but more loath to buy it at such a rate.

Of all men out of hell, none more to be

PRIDE AND WORLDLINESS 31

pitied than he that hangs over the mouth of it, and yet is fearless of his danger.

It requires courage to despise the shame which the Christian must expect to meet for his singularity, to avoid which many durst not confess Christ openly (John vii. 13). Many lose heaven because they are ashamed to go in a fool's coat thither. When the Christian must turn or burn, leave praying or become a prey, how many self-preserving distinctions would a cowardly heart invent? The Christian that hath so great opposition had need to be well locked into the saddle of his profession, or he will soon be dismounted.

IV

GLAD TIDINGS AND JOY

"Behold, I bring you good tidings of great joy, which shall be to all people. For unto you is born this day in the city of David a Saviour, which is Christ the Lord."—LUKE ii. 10, 11.

*I*NCARNATION. There is in Christ a foundation laid for greater familiarity with God than Adam was at first capable of. He, indeed, was the son of God, yet he was kept at a further distance, and treated with more state and majesty from God, than now the reconciled soul is; for though he was the son of God by creation, yet the Son of God was not then the Son of man by incarnation; and at this door comes in the believer's sweetest familiarity with God. God doth descend His throne, exchange His majestic robes of glory for man's frail flesh; He leaves His palace to live for a time in His creature's humble cottage, and there not only familiarly converses with him, but, which is stranger, ministers to him; yea, which is more than all these, He surrenders Himself up to endure all manner of indignities, from His sorry creature's hand. And when this coarse entertainment is done, back He posts to heaven, not to complain to His Father, how He hath been abused here below, and raise heaven's power against those who had so ill-treated Him, but to make ready heaven's palace for the reception of those who had thus abused Him, and now will accept of His grace. And lest these, yet left on earth, should fear His resumed royalty and majesty, in heaven's glory, would make some alteration with their affairs in His heart; to give them therefore a constant demonstration that He would be the same in the height of His honour that He was in the depth of His abasement, He goes back in the same clothes, to wear them on the throne, in all His glory, only some princely cost bestowed, to put them into the fashion of that heavenly kingdom, and make them suit with His glorified state;

giving them a pattern by this, what their own vile bodies, now so dishonourable, shall be made another day.

Redemption. Conscience requires as much to satisfy it as it doth to satisfy the justice of God Himself. But in the gospel, joyful news is brought to the sinner's ears of a fountain of blood there opened, which for its preciousness is as far above the price that divine justice demands for man's sin, as the blood of bulls and beasts was beneath it; and that is, the blood of Jesus Christ, who freely poured it upon the cross, and by it " obtained eternal redemption for us " (Heb. ix.). This is the door by which all true peace and joy comes into the conscience.

The simplicity of the gospel. If bread were as hard to come by as sweetmeats, or water as scarce as wine, the greatest part of men must needs famish; so if truths necessary to salvation were as hard to be understood, and cleared from Scriptures, as some others, many poor weak-hearted Christians would cer-

GLAD TIDINGS AND JOY

tainly perish without a miracle to help them. But the saving truths of the gospel lie plain, and run clear to all but those who muddy the streams with their own corrupt minds.

The abiding truth of the gospel. Consider God's especial care to preserve His truth; whatever is lost, God looks to His truth. In all the great revolutions, changes, and overturning of kingdoms, and churches also, God has still preserved His truth. In a word, in that great and dismal conflagration of heaven and earth, when the elements shall melt for heat, and the world come to its fatal period, then truth shall not suffer the least loss, but "the word of the Lord endureth for ever" (1 Pet. i. 25).

The peace of the gospel. "Let him take hold of My strength, that He may make peace with Me; and he shall make peace with Me" (Isa. xxvii. 5). And where lies God's saving strength, but in Christ? He hath laid strength upon this mighty One, able to save to the uttermost all that come to God by Him. Take hold of Christ, and thou hast hold of God's arm; He cannot strike the soul that holds thereby.

Where there is peace, such peace as peace with God and conscience, there can want no pleasure. David goes merry to bed, when he had nothing to supper but the gladness that God by this puts into his heart, and promiseth himself a better night's rest than any of them all, that are feasted with the world's cheer: "Thou hast put gladness in my heart, more than in the time that their corn and their wine increased. I will both lay me down in peace, and sleep" (Psa. iv. 7, 8). This same peace with God, enjoyed in the conscience, redounds to the comfort of the body. Now David can sleep sweetly, when he lies on a hard bed; what here he saith he would do, in Psalm iii. 5, he saith he hath done, "I laid me down and slept; I awaked; for the Lord sustained me." The title of the psalm tells us when David had this sweet night's rest; not when he lay on his bed of down in his stately palace at Jerusalem, but

GLAD TIDINGS AND JOY 37

when he fled for his life from his unnatural son Absalom, and possibly was forced to lie in the open field, under the canopy of heaven. . . . The great care which Christ took for His disciples, when He left the world, was not to leave them a quiet world to live in, but to arm them against a troublesome world : He bequeaths unto them His peace.

The rejection of the gospel. " Not one of those invited shall taste of my supper." God can least bear any contempt cast upon His grace. They would not come when the supper was on the table ; and therefore the cloth was drawn, and they go supperless to bed, and die in their sins. Christ thou wilt not, Christ therefore thou shalt not, have. None sink so deep in hell as those that fall into it with stumbling at Christ.

The joy of the gospel. Thy embracing Christ preached to thee in the gospel, will be as welcome news *to heaven,* I can tell thee, as the tidings of Christ and salvation through Him can be *to thee.* There is joy in heaven at the conversion of a sinner. Those angels that sang Christ into the world, will not want [lack] a song when He is received into thy heart, for He came into the world for this end.

Rejoice at the news: glad tidings, and sad hearts, do not go well together. When we see one heavy and sorrowful, we ask him what ill news he hath heard. Christian, what ill news hath Christ brought from heaven with Him that makes thee walk with thy folded arms and pensive countenance? "Saints shall shout aloud for joy" (Psa. cxxxii. 16). To see a wicked man merry and jocund, or a Christian sad and dumpish, is alike uncomely. . . . Truly the saint's heaviness reflects unkindly upon God Himself: we do not commend His cheer, if it doth not cheer us. O Christians, let the world see you are not losers in your joy, since you have been acquainted with the gospel; give them not cause to think by your uncomfortable walking, that when they turn Christians, they must bid all joy farewell, and resolve to spend their days in a house

GLAD TIDINGS AND JOY

of mourning. . . . Do not for shame, Christtian, run on the world's score by taking up any of its carnal joy; thou needest not go out of God's house to be merry. A Christian should deny himself of the world's joy and delights, lest they say, "These Christians draw their joy out of our cistern."

The saint's joy and peace is not such a light, frothy joy as the world's. The parlour wherein the Spirit of Christ entertains the Christian is an inner room, not next the street, for every one that goes by to smell the feast. "A stranger doth not intermeddle with his joy" (Prov. xiv. 10). Christ and the soul may be at supper within, and thou not so much as see one dish go in, or hear the music that sounds so sweetly in the Christian's ears. Perhaps thou thinkest he wants peace, because he doth not hang out a sign in his countenance of the joy and peace he hath within. Alas, poor wretch! may not the saint have a peaceful conscience, with a solemn, yea, sad countenance, as well as thou and thy companions have a

> For many, underneath the smile is tears.

40 GLEANINGS FROM THE PAST

sorrowful heart, when there is nothing but fair weather in your faces? "In laughter the heart is sorrowful" (Prov. xiv. 13).

The mystery of the gospel. As the gospel is a mystery of faith, it enables the godly to believe strange mysteries; to believe that which they understand not, and hope for that which they do not see. It teacheth them to believe that Christ was born in time, and that He was from everlasting; that He was comprehended in the Virgin's womb, and yet the heaven of heavens not able to contain Him: to be the Son of Mary, and yet her Maker; to be born without sin, and yet justly to have died for sin. They believe that God was just in punishing Christ, though innocent; and in justifying penitent believers, who are sinners; they believe themselves to be great sinners, and yet that God sees them in Christ without spot or wrinkle. Again, as the gospel is a mystery of godliness, it enables the godly to do as strange things as they believe; to live by Another's spirit, to act from Another's strength, to live to Another's will, and aim at Another's glory; they live by the Spirit of Christ, act with His strength, are determined by His will, and aim at His glory: it makes them so gentle, that a child may lead them to anything that is good; yet so stout, that fire shall not frighten them into sin: they can love their enemies, and yet, for Christ's sake, can hate father and mother: it makes them diligent in their worldly calling, yet enables them to condemn the riches they have obtained by God's blessing on their labour; they are taught by it that all things are theirs, yet they dare not take a pin from the wicked by force or fraud: it makes them so humble as to prefer every one above themselves; yet so to value their own condition, that the poorest among them would not change his estate with the greatest monarch of the world: it makes them thank God for health, and for sickness also; to rejoice when exalted, and not to repine when made low; they can pray for life, and at the same time desire to die! . . . The gospel opens a mine of unsearchable riches, but in a mystery; it shows men a way how to be rich in faith, rich in God, rich for another world, while poor in this. . . . Again the professors of the gospel are hated, because they partake of its mysterious nature. They are high-born, but in a mystery; you cannot see their birth by their outward breeding; arms they bear, and revenues they have to live on, but not such as the world judges the greatness of persons and families by: no, their outside is mean, while their inside is glorious; and the world values them by what they know and see of their external part, and not by their inward graces; they pass as princes in the disguise of some poor man's clothes through the world, and their entertainment is accordingly. Had Christ put on His robes of glory and majesty when He came into the world, surely He had not gone out of it with so shameful and cruel a death. The world would have trembled at His footstool, which some of them did, when but a beam of His deity looked forth upon them. Did saints walk on earth in those robes which they shall wear in heaven, then they would be feared and admired by those who now scorn and despise them. But as God's design in Christ's first coming would not have been fulfilled, had He so appeared; neither would His design in His saints, did the world know them as one day they shall; therefore He is pleased to let them lie hid under the mean coverings of poverty and infirmities, that so He may exercise their suffering graces, and also accomplish His wrath upon the wicked for theirs against them.

Is the gospel a mystery? then, Christian, long for heaven, and only there shall this mystery be fully known. Here we learn our knowledge of it by little and little, like one that reads a book as it comes from the press, sheet by sheet; there we shall see it altogether: here we learn with much pain and difficulty, there without travail and trouble: glorified saints, though they cease not from work, yet rest from labour: here passion blinds our minds, that we mistake error for truth, and truth for error; but these clouds shall be scattered and gone : here the weakness of natural parts keeps many in the dark, and renders them incapable of apprehending some truths, which others are led into ; but there the strong shall not prevent the weak, the scholar shall know as much as his master. . . . When that blessed hour comes, then lift up your heads with joy, for it will lead you into that blissful place where you will see Christ, not a great way off, not with the eye of faith, but with a glorified eye behold His very Person, never more to lose the sight of Him. Thou shalt no more hear what a glorious place heaven is, as thou were wont to have it set forth by the poor rhetoric of mortal man, preaching to thee of that with which he himself was little acquainted ; but shalt walk thyself in the streets of that glorious city, and bless thyself, to think what poor, low thoughts thou hadst thereof, when on earth thou didst meditate on this subject : one moment's sight of that glory will inform thee more than all the books written of it were ever able to do.

V

FAITH AND HOLINESS

" Without faith it is impossible to please Him."
>HEBREWS xi. 6.

" Follow peace with all . . . and holiness, without which no man shall see the Lord."
>HEBREWS xii. 14.

*F*AITH *in Christ.* Faith is that act of the soul whereby it rests on Christ crucified for pardon and life, and that upon the warrant of the word. The person of Christ is the object of faith as justifying: secondly, Christ as crucified. First, the person of Christ, not any axiom or proposition in the word;—this is the object of assurance, not of faith. Assurance saith, I believe my sins are pardoned through Christ: faith's language is, I believe on Christ for the pardon of them. . . . Not every one that assents to the truth of what Scripture saith of Christ doth believe on

Christ. This believing on Christ implies trusting recumbency on Christ. It is not the sight of a man's arm stretched out to a man in the water will save him from drowning, but the taking hold of it. "Let him *take hold* of my strength" (Isa. xxvii. 5).

"I know whom I have believed" (2 Tim. i. 12). None will readily trust a stranger that he is wholly unacquainted with. Abraham went indeed *he knew not whither*, but he did not go with *he knew not whom*.

Faith and repentance. Repentance, this is a sweet grace, but set on work by faith. Nineveh's repentance is attributed unto their faith (Jonah iii. 5): "The people of Nineveh believed God, and proclaimed a fast, and put on sackcloth." All is silence and quiet in an unbelieving soul: no news of repentance, no noise of any complaint made against sin, till faith begins to stir.

Faith and love. Love is another heavenly grace; but faith gathers the fuel that makes

FAITH AND HOLINESS

this fire. Speak, Christian, whose soul now flames with love to God, was it always thus? No, there was a time when thy hearth was cold, not a spark of this fire to be found on the altar of thy heart. How is it, then, Christian, that now thy soul loves God, whom before thou didst scorn and hate? Surely thou hast heard some good news from heaven, that hath changed thy thoughts of God, and turned the stream of thy love into this happy channel. And who can be the messenger besides faith, that brings any good news from heaven to thy soul? It is faith that proclaims the word, opens Christ's excellencies, pours out His name, for which the virgins love Him. When faith hath drawn a character of Christ out of the word, and presented Him in His love and loveliness to the soul, the Christian hath a copious theme to enlarge upon in his thoughts, whereby to endear Christ more and more to him. "Unto you therefore which believe He is precious" (1 Pet. ii. 7); and the more faith, the more precious.

Faith and a good conscience. " Holding faith, and a good conscience; which some having put away concerning faith have made shipwreck" (1 Tim. i. 19). Wouldst thou preserve thy faith, look to thy conscience. A good conscience is the bottom faith sails in; if the conscience be wrecked, how can it be thought that faith should be safe? If faith be the jewel, a good conscience is the cabinet in which it is kept; and if the cabinet be broken, the jewel must needs be in danger of losing.

The Christian's care should be to keep, as his conscience pure, so his name pure, which is done by avoiding all appearance of evil. Bernard's three questions are worth the asking ourselves in any enterprise: *An liceat? an deceat? an expediat?* "Is it lawful?" May I do it and not sin? "Is it becoming me, a Christian?" May I do it and not wrong my profession? Lastly, "Is it expedient?" May I do it and not offend my weak brother?

FAITH AND HOLINESS 49

Faith and prayer. True faith is prayerful; prayer is the child of faith. As the creature cannot pray *without* faith, so *with* faith he cannot but pray. The new creature (like our infants in their natural birth) comes crying into the world : and therefore Christ tells it for great news to Ananias of Saul, a new-born believer, " Behold, he prayeth ! "

Faith enables the soul to persevere in prayer. "Will [the hypocrite] always call upon God ? " (Job xxvii. 10). No, he prays himself weary of praying ; something or other will in time make him quarrel with that which he never inwardly liked ; whereas the sincere believer hath that in him which makes it impossible he should quite give over praying, except he should also cease believing : prayer is the very breath of faith ; stop a man's breath, and where is he then ?

Faith may live in a storm, but it will not suffer a storm to live in it. As faith rises, so the blustering wind of the discontented troublesome thoughts go down. Faith relieves the soul in prayer of that which oppresses it; whereas the unbelieving soul still carries about it the cause of its troubles, because it had not strength to cast forth its sorrows and roll its cares upon God.

Weak faith. Weak faith will as surely land the Christian in heaven as strong faith; but the weak, doubting Christian is not like to have so pleasant a voyage thither as another with strong faith. Though all in the ship come safe to shore, yet he that is all the way seasick hath not so comfortable a voyage as he that is strong and healthful.

As melancholy men delight in melancholy walks, so doubting souls most frequent such places of Scripture in their musing thoughts as increase their doubts.

"Why are ye fearful, O ye of little faith!" (Matt. viii. 26). You see the leak at which the water came in to sink their spirits: they had "little faith." It is not what God is in Himself, but what our apprehensions

FAITH AND HOLINESS

at present are of God, that pacifies and comforts a soul in great straits. If a man fear the house will fall on his head in a storm though it be as immovable as a rock, yet that will not ease his mind till he thinks it so.

Bold faith. "I will never leave thee, nor forsake thee" (Heb. xiii. 5)—there is the promise; and the inference, which he teacheth us to draw by faith from this, follows (ver. 6), "So that we may boldly say, The Lord is my helper." We may boldly assert it in the face of men and devils, because He that is almighty hath said it.

Faith is a right pilgrim-grace; it travels with us to heaven, and when it sees us safe got within our Father's doors it takes leave of us.

Holiness and happiness. "He hath chosen us in Him before the foundation of the world, that we should be holy" (Eph. i. 4). Mark, not because He foresaw that they would be of themselves holy, but that they should be holy; this was that God resolved He would make them to be. Consider it is not necessary that thou shouldst be rich; but it is necessary thou shouldst be holy, if thou meanest to be happy. You may travel to heaven with never a penny in your purse, but not without holiness in your heart and life also.

→ I. Tim. 4:4

Holiness and contentment. "Godliness with content is great gain." The holy person is the only contented man in the world. Paul tells us "he had learnt in whatsoever state he was to be content."

Holiness in the home. It is in vain to talk of holiness if we can bring no letters testimonial from our holy walking with our relations. O, it is sad when they that have reason to know us best, by their daily converse with us, do speak least for our godliness! Few so impudent as to come naked into the streets: if men have anything to cover their naughtiness they will put it on

FAITH AND HOLINESS 53

when they come abroad. But what art thou within doors? Pray not only against the power of sin, but for the power of holiness. His zeal is false that seems hot against sin, but is cold to holiness.

VI

WILES AND TEMPTATIONS

"There hath no temptation taken you but such as is common to man: but God is faithful, who will not suffer you to be tempted above that ye are able; but will with the temptation also make a way to escape, that ye may be able to bear it."

1 CORINTHIANS x. 13.

THE Devil's dupes. Many have yielded to go a mile with Satan, that never intended to go two. Thus Satan leads poor creatures down into the depths of sin by winding stairs, that let them not see the bottom whither they are going: first, he presents an object that occasions some thoughts, these set the affections on fire, and these fume up into the brain and cloud the understanding, which, being thus disabled, now Satan dares a little more declare himself, and boldly solicit the creature to that it would otherwise have defied. Give not place to Satan! no, not an inch in his first motions; he that is a beggar, and a modest one without doors, will command the house if let in.

The devil teaches sinners to cover foul practices with fair names—superstition must be styled devotion; covetousness, thrift; pride in apparel, handsomeness; looseness, liberty; and madness, mirth.

The Devil's wiles. Satan makes choice of such as have a great name for holiness: none like a live bird to draw other birds into the net. Abraham tempts his wife to lie: " Say thou art my sister." The old prophet leads the man of God out of his way (1 Kings xiii).

Under the skirt of Christian liberty Satan conveys in libertinism; by crying up the Spirit he decries and vilifies the Scripture; by magnifying faith, he labours to undermine repentance and blow up good works.

If Satan get into thy spirit and defile it, O, how hard wilt thou find it to stay there? Thou hast already sipped of his broth, and now are more likely to sit down and make thy full meal of that, which by tasting hath vitiated thy palate already.

When you hear one commend another for a wise or good man, and at last come in with a "but" that dasheth all, you will easily think he is no friend to the man, but some sly enemy, that by seeming to commend, desires to disgrace the more. Thus, when you find God represented to you as merciful and gracious, but not to such a great sinner as you; to have power and strength, but not able to save thee; you may say, Avaunt, Satan, thy speech bewrayeth thee.

When the flesh or Satan beg time *of* thee, it is to steal time *from* thee. They put thee off prayer at one time, to shut thee out at last from prayer at any time.

What day in all the year is inconvenient

WILES AND TEMPTATIONS 57

to Satan ? What place or company art thou in, that he cannot make a snare for thy soul ?

Satan knows what orders thou keepest in thy house and closet; and though he hath not a key to thy heart, yet he can stand in the next room to it, and lightly hear what is whispered there. If once he doth but smell which way thy heart inclines, he knows how to take the hint; if but one door is unbolted, here is advantage enough.

The occasion of temptation. The least passage of thy life may prove an occasion of sin to thee: at what a little wicket many times a great sin enters! David's eye did but casually light on Bathsheba, and the good man's foot was presently in the devil's trap: hast thou not then need to pray that God would set a guard about thy senses wherever thou goest, and to cry with him, "Keep back mine eyes from beholding vanity"?

It should be our care, if we would not yield to the sin, not to walk by, or sit at the door of the occasion : parley not with that in thy thoughts, which thou meanest not to let into thy heart. If we mean not to be burnt, let us not walk upon the coals of temptation. Thou temptest God to suffer thy locks to be cut, when thou art so bold as to lay thy head in the lap of a temptation.

Set a strong guard about thy outward senses : these are Satan's landing-places, especially the eye and the ear. Take heed what thou importest at these ; vain discourse seldom passeth without leaving some tincture upon the heart. And for thy eye, let it not wander ; wanton objects cause wanton thoughts. Job knew his eye and his thoughts were like to go together, and therefore to secure one he covenants with the other (Job xxxi. 1).

The haft of Satan's hatchet, with which he lies chopping at the root of the Christian's comfort, is commonly made of the

WILES AND TEMPTATIONS

Christian's wood. First, he tempts to sin, and then for it. Satan is but a creature, and cannot work without tools; he can indeed make much of little, but not anything of nothing, as we see in his assaulting of Christ, where he troubled himself to little purpose, because he came and found nothing in Him (John xiv. 30). Though the devil throws the stone, it is the mud in us that disturbs our comfort.

Be sure thou art watchful more than ordinary over thyself, in those things where thou findest thyself weakest and hast been oftenest foiled. The weakest part of a city needs the strongest guard.

The devil would tempt Christ when he " shewed Him all the kingdoms of the world," and promised them all unto Him, if He would " fall down and worship Him." Everyone that by unrighteousness doth seek the world's pelf goes to the devil for it, and doth worship him in effect. How much better it is to have poverty from God than riches from the devil! A temptation comes strong, when the way to relief seems to lie through the sin that Satan is wooing to: when one is poor, and Satan comes, "What, wilt starve rather than step over the hedge, and steal for thy supply?" This is enough to put flesh and blood to the stand.

Deliverance from temptation. What saith thy soul, when God hedgeth up thy way, and keeps thee from that sin which Satan hath been soliciting for? If on Christ's side, thou wilt rejoice when thou art delivered out of a temptation, though it be by falling into an affliction.

Christian, it is ill done of thee to make a breach in thy holy course, by tampering with any sin; but thou wilt commit a greater if thou turnest thy back on God also when thou shouldst humble thyself for thy former sin. Thou hast fallen into sin in the day, wilt thou not, therefore, pray at night? Take heed thou run not farther into temptation. Now is the time for the devil to set

WILES AND TEMPTATIONS

upon thee, when the weapon of prayer is out of thy hand. The best thou canst look for is a storm from God to bring thee back again, and the sooner it comes the more merciful He is to thee.

"Watch and pray," saith our Saviour, "that ye enter not into temptation" (Matt. xxvi. 41). They, not keeping this pass, gave the enemy, Satan, a fair occasion to come in upon them; and as they were led into temptation by neglect of prayer, so they were rescued and led out of it again by Christ's prayer, which He mercifully laid in beforehand for them: "I have prayed for thee, that thy faith fail not."

Let this encourage thee, O Christian, in thy conflict with Satan; the skirmish may be sharp, but it cannot be long. The cloud, while it drops, is rolling over thy head, and then comes fair weather, and eternal sunshine of glory.

Thou canst not be long off thy watch, but

the devil will hear on it. The devil knew the apostle's sleeping time, and then he desires leave to winnow them (Luke xxii.). The thief riseth when honest men go to bed. The devil begins to tempt when saints cease to watch. . . . The saint's sleeping time is Satan's tempting time; every fly dares venture to creep on a sleeping lion. No temptation so weak but is strong enough to foil a Christian that is napping in security. Samson asleep, and Delilah cut his locks. Saul asleep, and the spear is taken away from his very side, and he never the wiser. Noah asleep, and his graceless son has a fit time to discover his father's nakedness. Eutychus asleep, nods, and falls from the third loft, and is taken up for dead. The Christian asleep may soon lose his spiritual strength, be robbed of his spear, and his nakedness discovered by graceless men, to the shame of his profession. Yea, he may fall from a high loft of profession, so low, into scandalous practices, that others may question whether there be any life of grace in him.

WILES AND TEMPTATIONS

The Christian's safety lies in resisting. All the armour provided is to defend the Christian fighting, none to secure him flying; stand, and the day is ours; fly, or yield, and all is lost.

VII

SUFFERING AND SHAME

"The sufferings of this present time are not worthy to be compared with the glory that shall be revealed in us."—ROMANS viii. 18.

SUFFERING for Christ. "Unto you it is given in the behalf of Christ, not only to believe on Him, but also to suffer for His sake" (Phil. i. 29). All the parts and common gifts that a man hath will never enable him to drink deep of this cup for Christ; such is the pride of man's heart, he had rather suffer any way than this; rather from himself, and for himself, than from Christ, or for Christ. You would wonder to see sometimes how much a child will endure at his play, and never cry for it: this fall, and that knock, and no great matter is made of it by him, because got in a way that is pleasing to him; but let his father whip

SUFFERING AND SHAME 65

him, though it put him not to half the smart, yet he roars and takes on, that there is no quieting of him.

Most men are more tender of their skin than of their conscience, and had rather the gospel had provided armour to defend their bodies from death and danger, than their souls from sin and Satan. All the pieces are to defend the Christian from sin: none to secure him from suffering. Here is the true reason why so few come at the beat of Christ's drum to His standard, and so many of those few that have enlisted themselves by an external profession under Him, within a while drop away, and leave His colours; it is suffering work they are sick of.

Sufferings for the gospel are no matter of shame. Paul doth not blush to tell, it is for the gospel he is in bonds. The shame belonged to them that put on the chain, not to him that wore it. "If any man suffer as a Christian, let him not be ashamed, but let him glorify God on this behalf" (1 Peter iv.

16). The apostles rejoiced that "they were counted worthy to suffer shame for His name" (Acts v. 41). Shall the wicked glory in their shame, and thou be ashamed of thy glory?

Heaven is but little worth if thou hast not a heart to despise a little shame, and bear a few taunts from profane Ishmaels for thy hopes of it. Let them spit on thy face, Christ will wipe it off; let them laugh, so thou winnest.

Fear not what you can suffer, only be careful for what you suffer. Christ's cross is made of sweet wood; there are comforts peculiar to those who suffer for righteousness. The true cause of Paul's sufferings was his zeal for God and His truth; "For which I am in bonds." That is, for the gospel which I profess and preach: as that martyr, who being asked how he came to prison, showed his Bible, and said, "This brought me hither." Persecutors may pretend what they please, but it is the saint's religion and piety that their spite is at.

Blessing through suffering. Persecution doth but mow the church, which afterward comes up the thicker for it; it is unholiness that ruins it. Persecutors do but plough God's field for Him, while He is sowing it with the blood that they let out. Few are made better by prosperity, whom afflictions make worse. He that will sin, though he goes in pain, will much more if that be gone.

Prepared for suffering. The proverb is, He that would learn to pray let him go to sea; but I think it were better thus, He that would go to sea (this I mean of suffering) let him learn to pray before he comes there.

Christian, suffering may overtake thee suddenly; therefore be ready shod. Sometimes orders come to soldiers for a sudden march; they must be gone as soon as the drum beats. And so mayest thou be called out, before thou art aware, to suffer for God or from God. Abraham had little time given him to deal with his heart, and persuade it into a compliance with God, for offering his son Isaac; a great trial and short warning: "Take now thy son, thine only son Isaac" (Gen. xxii. 2). Not a year, a month, a week hence, but now! This was in the night, and Abraham is gone early in the morning. How couldst thou, in thy perfect strength and health, endure to hear the message of death, if God should, before any lingering sickness hath brought thee into some acquaintance with death, say no more, but, Up and die, as once to Moses? Art thou shod for such a journey? Couldst thou say, " Good is the word of the Lord "?

" The children of Ephraim, being armed, and carrying bows, turned back in the day of battle" (Ps. lxxviii. 9). Why? What is the matter? So well armed, and yet so cowardly? This seems strange: read the preceding verse, and you will cease wondering; they are called there, "a generation that set not their heart aright, and whose spirit was not stedfast with God."

Be sure thou givest up thy lust to the sword of the Spirit, before thy life is in danger from the sword of the persecutor. Canst thou be willing to lay down thy life for Christ, and yet keep an enemy in thy bosom out of the hand of justice, that seeks to take away the life of Christ ? Persecutors tempt as well as torture. It is possible for one to die in the cause of Christ, and not be His martyr. Thy heart must be holy which thou sufferest with, as well as the cause thou sufferest for. He alone is Christ's martyr, that suffers for Christ. "If, when ye do well, and suffer for it, ye take it patiently, this is acceptable with God ; for even hereunto were ye called ; because Christ also suffered for us, leaving us an example, that ye should follow His steps ; . . . who, when He was reviled, reviled not again ; when He suffered, He threatened not " (1 Peter ii. 20-23). This is hard work indeed, in the very fire to keep the spirits cool, and clear of wrath and revenge. But it makes him that by grace can do it, a glorious conqueror. Flesh and blood would bid a man call fire from heaven, rather than mercy to fall upon them that so cruelly handle him. He that can forgive his enemy is too hard for him, and hath the better of him; because his enemy's blows do not bruise his flesh, but the wounds that love gives, pierce the conscience.

Many that never could be beaten from the truth by dint of argument, have been forced from it by fire of persecution. It is not an orthodox judgment will enable a man to suffer for the truth at the stake.

Fellowship in sufferings. This would speak grace high in its exercise when a person is himself swimming in the abundance of all enjoyments, and can then lay aside his own joy to weep and mourn for and with any afflicted saints. It is not usual for any but those of great grace to feel the cords of the church's afflictions through a bed of down;

SUFFERING AND SHAME

it must be a David that can prefer Jerusalem above his chief joy. On the other hand, when in the depths of our own personal troubles, we can yet reserve a large space in our prayers for other saints, bespeaks a great measure of grace. When in our distresses we can entertain the tidings of any other saint's mercies with joy and thankfulness; this requires great grace. The prosperity of others too often breeds envy in them that want it; if, therefore, thou canst praise God for mercies granted to others while the tears stand in thy eyes for thine own miseries, it is what flesh and blood never learnt thee.

"Fear not them which kill the body, but are not able to kill the soul : but rather fear Him which is able to destroy both soul and body in hell" (Matt. x. 28). Children are afraid of bugbears, that cannot hurt them ; but they can play with fire that will burn them ; and no less childish is it to be frightened into a sin at the frown of a man, who hath no power to hurt us more than our own fear gives him; and to play with hell-fire into which God is able to cast us for ever. What was John Huss the worse for his fool's cap that his enemies put on his head, so long as under it he had a helmet of hope, which they could not take off? Or how much the nearer hell was the same blessed martyr for their committing his soul to the devil? No nearer than some of their own are to heaven, for being sainted in the Pope's Calendar.

Sustained in suffering. None find such quick despatch at the throne of grace as suffering saints. "In the day when I cried," saith David, "thou answeredst me, and strengthenedst me with strength in my soul" (Ps. cxxxviii. 3). Peter knocked at the gate, who were assembled to seek God for him, almost as soon as their prayer knocked at heaven's gate in his behalf. There is ever a door more than the Christian sees in his prison, by which Christ can with a turn of His hand open a way for His saint's escape. Man may, the devil to be sure will, leave all

SUFFERING AND SHAME 73

in the lurch that do his work. But if God sets thee on He will bring thee off; never fear a "look thee to that" from His lips, when thy faithfulness to Him hath brought thee into the briers: only be not troubled if thou art cast overboard, like Jonah, before thou seest the provision which God makes for thy safety: it is ever at hand, but sometimes out of sight, like Jonah's whale, sent of God to ferry him ashore under water, and the prophet in his belly, before he knew where he was. That which thou thinkest come to devour thee, may be the messenger that God sends to bring thee safe to land.

The Egyptians thought they had Israel in a trap, when they saw them by the seaside. When they are out of danger, behold they are in a wilderness, where nothing is to be had for back or belly, and yet here they shall live forty years, without trade or tillage, without begging or robbing of any of the neighbour nations; they shall not be beholden to them for a penny in their way. What cannot almighty power do to provide for His people.

"The Lord is my portion, saith my soul; therefore will I hope in Him" (Lam. iii. 24). Hast thou not chosen Him for thy portion? Dost thou not look for a heaven to enjoy Him in for ever? And can any dungeon of outward affliction be so dark, that this hope will not enlighten? He that hath laid up a portion in heaven for thee, will lay out surely all the expenses thou needest in thy way thither. Remember how often God hath confuted thy fears, and proved thy unbelief a false prophet. Hath He not knocked at thy door with inward comfort and outward deliverance, when thou hadst put out the candle of hope, given over looking for Him, and been ready to lay thyself down on the bed of despair? Wert thou never at so sad a pass, the storm of thy fears so great that the anchor of hope even came home, and left thee to feed with misgiving and despairing thoughts, as if now thy everlasting night were come, and no morning

SUFFERING AND SHAME 75

supply expected by thee ? Yet even then thy God proved them all liars, by an unlooked-for surprise of mercy, with which He stole sweetly in upon thee.

Suffering and glory. There are few who are greedy hunters after the world's enjoyments, that do drive their worldly trade without running in debt to their consciences. And I am sure he buys gold too dear, that pays the peace of his conscience for the purchase. But heaven is had cheap, though it be with the loss of all our carnal interests, even life itself.

" Ought not Christ to have suffered these things, and to enter into His glory ? " (Luke xxiv. 26). And truly the saints' way to salvation lies in the same road (Rom. viii. 17) : "If so be that we suffer with Him, that we may be also glorified together," only with this advantage, that His going before hath beaten it plain, so that now it may be forded, which but for Him had been utterly impassable to us.

O comfort one another, Christians, with this! though your life be evil with troubles, yet it is short; a few steps, and you are out of the rain. There is a great difference between a saint, in regard of the evils he meets with, and the wicked; as two travellers riding contrary ways, both taken in the rain and wet, but one rides from the rain, and so is soon out of the shower; but the other rides into the rainy corner, the further he goes the worse he is. The saint meets with trouble as well as the wicked, but he is soon out of the shower; but as for the wicked, the further he goes the worse: what he meets with here is but a few drops, the great storm is the last.

When the Christian's affairs are most disconsolate, he may soon meet with a happy change. The joy of that blessed day comes "in a moment, in the twinkling of an eye . . . we shall be changed" (1 Cor. xv. 52). In one moment sick and sad, in the next well and glad, never to know more what groans and tears mean. Now clad with the

SUFFERING AND SHAME

rags of mortal flesh, made miserable with a thousand troubles that attend it, in the twinkling of an eye arrayed with the robes of immortality, enriched with a thousand times more glory than the sun itself wears in that garment of light which now dazzleth our eyes. Who can wonder to see a saint cheerful in his afflictions, that knows what good news he expects to hear from heaven, and how soon he knows not? The saints' hope is laid up in heaven, and yet it heals all the wounds which they receive on earth. If Christ sends his disciples to sea, He means to be with them when they most need His company. "When thou passest through the waters, I will be with thee" (Isa. xliii. 2).

VIII

STRIFE AND CONTENTION

"Spoiling and violence are before me: and there are that raise up strife and contention."
HABAKKUK i. 3.

CONTENTION is uncomfortable, with whomsoever we fall out: neighbours or friends, wife or husband, children or servants; but worst of all with God.

Consider the unhappy contentions and divisions that are found among the people of God. Contentions ever portend ill. Christ sets up the light of His gospel to walk and work by, not to fight and wrangle; and therefore, it were no wonder, at all if He should put it out, and so end the dispute. If these storms which have been of late years upon us, and are not yet off, had but made Christians, as that did the disciples (Mark vi. 48), ply their oars, and lovingly row all one way, it had been happy ; we might then have expected Christ to come walking toward us in mercy, and help us safe to land ; but when we throw away the oar, and fall to strife in the ship, while the wind continues loud about us, truly we are more likely to drive Christ from us, than to invite Him to us ; we are in a more probable way of sinking than saving of the ship and ourselves in it.

There is nothing (next to Christ and heaven) that the devil grudges believers more than their peace and mutual love : if he cannot rend them from Christ, stop them from getting heaven, yet he takes some pleasure to see them go thither in a storm, like a shattered fleet severed from one another, that they may have no assistance from, nor comfort of each other's company all the way. One ship is easier taken than a squadron.

If the gospel will not allow us to pay our enemies in their own coin, and give them wrath for wrath, much less will it suffer brethren to spit fire at one another's face.

When children fight and wrangle, now is the time they may expect their father to come and part them with his rod. "He shall turn the heart of the fathers to the children, and the heart of the children to their fathers, lest I come and smite the earth with a curse" (Mal. iv. 6). Strife and contention set a people next door to a curse. God brings a heavy judgment upon a people when Himself leaves them. "Be of one mind," saith the apostle, "live in peace; and the God of love and peace shalt be with you" (2 Cor. xiii. 11), implying that if they did not live in peace they must not look to have His company long with them.

In our divided times, wherein there is so much difference of judgment, had there been less wrangling among ourselves and more wrestling with God, we had been in a fairer way to find the door of truth, which so many are yet groping for. The way of controversy is dusty, and contentious disputes raiseth this dust, and blows it most into their eyes that gallop fastest in it, so that they miss the truth, which humble souls find upon their knees at the throne of grace. . . . Sinning times have ever been the saint's praying times : this sent Ezra with a heavy heart to confess the sin of his people (Ezra ix.) And Jeremiah tells the wicked of his degenerate age that his " soul should weep in secret places for their pride " (Jer. xiii. 17).

" The love of many shall wax cold," and no wonder when self-love waxeth so hot. It was foretold also by the apostle (2 Tim. iii. 1, 2), " In the last days . . . men shall be lovers of their own selves "; and what a black regiment follows this captain, sin ! If once a man makes self the whole of his aim, farewell loving of, or praying for others : charity cannot dwell in so narrow a house as the self-lover's heart ; yea, it is opposed to it : " Love seeketh not her own " (1 Cor. xiii. 5).

They were none of the best Christians of whom Paul gives this character, "They sought their own." As the heart advances in grace, so it grows more public-spirited: the higher a man ascends a hill, the larger will be his prospect: his eye is not confined within the compass of his own wall. The carnal spirit thinks of none but himself; whereas grace elevates the soul, and the more grace a man hath, the more it will enable him to look from himself into the condition of his brethren.

I have known one that when he had some envious unkind thoughts stirring in him, against any one (and who so holy as may not find such vermin sometimes creeping about him), he would go to the throne of grace where he would most earnestly pray for the increase of those good things in them which he before had seemed to grudge.

When love hath once laid the dust which passion and prejudice have blown in our eyes, we shall then stand at greater advan-

STRIFE AND CONTENTION 83

tage for finding out truth. Pity thy weak brother, and take him by the hand for his help, but despise him not ; God can make him to stand and suffer thee to fall : Christ doth not quench the smoking flax—why should we ?

The persecutor's sword is not at the church's throat among us ; but are not Christians falling out among themselves ? The question hath often been asked, why the word preached hath been no more effectual to convert the wicked, or to edify the saints ? One of the chief causes is the divisions amongst those that have made the greatest profession of the truth. The body of Christ is edified by love (Eph. iv. 16). The apostles themselves, when wrangling got little good by Christ's sermon, or the supper itself, administered by Christ unto them. One would have thought that was such a meal, in the strength whereof (as so many Elijahs) they might have gone a long journey ; but, alas ! we see how weak they arise from it ; one denies his Master, and the rest in alarm forsake Him. Christ prays for His people's unity, "That the world may believe that thou hast sent me "(John xvii. 21). This should stir up all that wish well to the gospel, to pray for the reunion of divided hearts; hot disputes will not do it; prayer will, or nothing can. The God of peace can only set us at peace : if ever we are wise to agree, we must obtain our wisdom from above; this alone is pure and peaceable.

The unreasonableness of the strife betwixt Abraham's herdsmen and Lot's is aggravated by the near neighbourhood of the heathens to them, " And there was a strife between the herdmen of Abram's cattle and the herdmen of Lot's cattle : and the Canaanite and Perizzite dwelled then in the land " (Gen. xiii. 7). . . . O Christians, shall Herod and Pilate put you to shame ? They clapped up a peace to strengthen their hands against Christ; and will not you unite against your common enemy ? . . . Contentions put a stop to the growth of grace. The body may as well thrive in a fever, as the soul prosper when on a flame with strife and contention. Observe that place (Eph. iv. 15): "But speaking the truth in love," or being sincere in love, "may grow up into Him in all things." The apostle is upon a cure, showing how souls may come to thrive and flourish; and the receipt he gives is a composition of these two rare drugs, sincerity and love; preserve these and all will go well. There may be preaching, but no edifying, without love. You cut off your trade with heaven, at the throne of grace; you will be little *in prayer* to God, if much *in squabbling* with your brethren. It is impossible to go from wrangling to praying, with a free spirit. And if you should be so bold as to knock at God's door, you are sure to have cold welcome, "Leave there thy gift before the altar, and go thy way; first be reconciled to thy brother, and then come and offer thy gift." As we cut off our trade with heaven, so with one another; when two countries fall out they must needs both pinch by the war. No Christian could well live without borrowing from his brethren. There is that "which every joint supplieth according to the effectual working in the measure of every part" (Eph. iv. 16). Contentions and divisions spoil all intercourse among believers. Communication flows from communion, and communion is founded upon union. The church grows under persecution; that sheds the seed all over the field, and brings the gospel where else it had not been heard of; but divisions and contentions, like a furious storm, washes the seed out of the land, with its heart, fatness, and all. Contentions not only hazard the decay of grace, but growth of sin. "If ye have bitter envying, and strife in your hearts, glory not; . . . for where envying and strife is, there is confusion and every evil work." Contention is the devil's forge, in which if he can but give a Christian a heat or two, he will soften him for his hammer of temptation. Moses himself, when his spirit was a little hot, "spake unadvisedly with his lips."

We are prone to mistake our heat for zeal, whereas commonly in strife between saints it is a fire-ship sent in by Satan to break their unity and order; wherein while they stand they are an armada invincible: and Satan knows he hath no other way but this to shatter them: when the Christian's language, which should be one, begins to be confounded, they are then near scattering.

Was there ever less love, charity, self-denial, heavenly mindedness, or the power of holiness, than in this sad age of ours? Alas! these are in great danger of perishing in the fire of contention and division, which a perverse zeal in less things hath kindled among us.

Lay this deep in thy heart, that God, which gives an eye to see truth, must give a hand to hold it fast when we have it. What we have from God we cannot keep without God; keep therefore thy acquaintance with God, or else truth will not keep her acquaintance long with thee. God is light: thou art going into the dark, as soon as thou turnest thy back upon Him. We stand at better advantage to find truth, and keep it also, when devoutly praying for it, than fiercely wrangling and contending about it : disputes toil the soul and raise the dust of passion ; prayer sweetly composeth the mind, and lays the passions which disputes draw forth ; and I am sure a man may see further in a still, clear day, than in a windy and cloudy. When a person talks much and rests little, we have great cause to fear his brain will not long hold out ; and truly, when a person shall be much in talking and disputing about truth, without a humble spirit in prayer to be led into it, God may justly punish that man's pride with a spiritual frenzy in his mind, that he shall not know error from truth.

A truth under dispute is stopped in the head : it cannot commence in the heart, or become practicable in the life.

Many a sharp conflict there hath been between saint and saint, scuffling in the dark through misunderstanding of the truth and each other.

There is a day coming, and it cannot be far from us, in which we shall meet lovingly in heaven, and sit at one feast : full fruition of God shall be the feast, and peace and love the sweet music that shall sound to it ; and what folly it is for us to *fight* here who shall *feast* there !

IX

SERVANTS AND SERVICE

"He that hath My word, let him speak My word faithfully. What is the chaff to the wheat? saith the Lord."—JEREMIAH xxiii. 28.

*P*REACH *the truth.* Take heed of giving thy own dreams and fancies in God's name. All is chaff except the pure word of God. O stamp not God's image on thine own coin! We live in high-flown times : many people are not content with truths that lie plainly in the Scriptures ; and some, to please their wanton palates, have sublimated their notions so high, that they have flown out of the sight of the Scripture, and unawares run themselves, with others, into dangerous errors. Make not experiments upon the souls of people, by delivering what is doubtful. Better feed people with sound doctrine though it be a plain meal, than that thou

SERVANTS AND SERVICE

shouldst, with an outlandish dish, light on a wild gourd, that brings death into their pot.

Preach with the fear of God. A little bread, with God's blessing, may make a meal for a multitude ; and great provision may soon shrink to nothing, if God help not in the breaking of it. It is not thy sermon in thy head, or notes in thy book, that will enable thee to preach, except God open thy mouth ; acknowledge, therefore, God in all thy ways, and lean not to thy own understanding : the swelling of the heart, as well as of the wall, goes before a fall. How much may it provoke God, when thou goest to the pulpit, and passest by his door in the way, without calling for His assistance ? . . . Not only the preparation of the heart, but the answer of the tongue, both are from the Lord (Prov. xvi. 1). God keeps the key of the mouth as well of the heart ; not a word can be uttered, until God opens the door of the lips to give it a free egress. He opened the mouth of the ass, and stopped the mouth of that wicked prophet, its master (Num. xxii. 28–31) : hear him confess as much to Balak : " Lo, I am come unto thee : have I now any power at all to say anything ? the word that God putteth in my mouth, that shall I speak " (verse 38).

Preach without fear of man. There is nothing more unworthy than to see a people bold to sin, and the preacher afraid to reprove them. It is said of Tacitus, that he took the same liberty to write the emperors' lives, that they took in leading them.

Man-pleasing is both endless and needless. If thou wouldst thou couldst not please all ; and if thou couldst, there is no need, if thou pleasest Him that can turn all their hearts and bind their hands. They speed best that dare be faithful. Jonah was afraid of his work : O, he durst not go to such a great city with such a sad message : to tell them that they should be destroyed, was to set them at work to destroy him that brought the news ; but how near was he to losing his life by running away to save it? Jeremiah seemed the only man likely to lose his life by his bold preaching; yet he had fairer quarter at last than the smooth preachers of his time. If thou art free and bold, thou mayest, indeed, be *mocked* by some, but thou wilt be *reverenced* by more: yea, even they that wag their heads at thee, carry that in their conscience which will make them' fear thee: they are the flattering preachers who become base among the people (Mal. ii. 9). It is not wisdom to provoke the judge, by flattering the prisoner.

Where one saith, How shall I do this and sin against God? many in their hearts say, How shall I do this and anger man? Herod feared John, and did many things; had he feared God he would have laboured to have done everything.

Fall to the work God sets thee about, and thou engagest His strength for thee. "The way of the Lord is strength." Run from thy work and thou engagest God's strength against thee; He will send some storm or other after thee to bring home His runaway servant. How oft hath the coward been killed in a ditch, or under some hedge, when the valiant soldier that stood his ground and kept his place, got off with safety and honours?

Preach with a good conscience. Keep a clear conscience: he cannot be a bold reprover, that is not a conscientious liver; such a one must speak softly, for fear of waking his own guilty conscience. Unholiness in the preacher's life, either will stop his mouth from *reproving*, or the people's ears from *receiving*. O how harsh a sound does such a cracked bell make in the ears of his auditors!

Preach definitely. He is the better workman, who drives one nail home with reiterated blows, than he which covets to enter many, but fastens none. Such preachers are not likely to reach the conscience, who hop from one truth to another,

SERVANTS AND SERVICE 95

but dwell on none. Were I to buy a garment in a shop, I should like him better that lays one good piece or two before me that are for my turn, which I may fully examine, than him who takes down all his shop, and heaps piece upon piece, merely to show his store, till at last for variety I can look attentively on none, they lie so one upon another.

Preach faithfully. The preacher must read and study people as diligently as any book in his study; and as he finds them, dispense like a faithful steward unto them. People complain, we are so oft reproving the same error or sin; and the fault is their own, because they will not leave it. Who will blame the dog for continuing to bark, when the thief is all the while in the yard? Alas, alas, it is not once or twice rousing against sin will do it!

" It is required in stewards, that a man be found faithful " (1 Cor. iv. 2). The preacher's faithfulness stands in relation to him that intrusts him. It is very unlikely that a steward, in giving out provision, should please all the servants in the house; such officers have least thanks when they do their work best. He that thinks to please men, goes about an endless and needless work. A wise physician seeks to *cure*, not to *please* his patient. He that chides when he is sick, for the bitterness of the potions, will give thee thanks for it when he is recovered.

Preach simply. The word of God is too sacred a thing, and preaching too solemn a work, to be toyed and played with, as is the usage of some, who make a sermon but matter of wit and fine oratory. Their sermon is like a child's doll, from which if you take its dress, the rest is worth nothing. It is well indeed when the people can keep pace with the preacher. To preach truths and notions above the hearers' capacity, is like a nurse that should go to feed a child with a spoon too big to go into its mouth.

Preach wisely. " Because the preacher was wise, he . . . sought to find out acceptable words " (Eccles. xii. 9, 10). Not rude, loose, and indigested stuff, in a slovenly manner brought forth, lest the sluttery of the cook should turn the stomachs of the guests.

Preach gently. " The servant of the Lord must not strive ; but be gentle unto all, apt to teach, patient, in meekness instructing those that oppose themselves " (2 Tim. ii. 24, 25). O how careful is God that nothing should be in the preacher to prejudice the sinner's judgment, or harden his heart against the offer of His grace ! If the servant be proud and hasty, how shall they know that the Master is meek and patient ? He that will take the bird must not scare it. A forward, peevish messenger is no friend to him that sends him. Sinners are not pelted into Christ with stones of hard provoking language, but wooed into Christ by heart-melting exhortations.

The oil makes the nail drive without splitting the board. The word never enters the heart more kindly, than when it falls most gently: "Ride prosperously, because of truth and meekness" (Ps. xlv. 4). Be as rough to thy people's sins as thou canst, so thou be gentle to their souls. Dost thou take the rod of reproof into thine hand? Let them see that love, not wrath, gives the blow. The word preached comes, indeed, best from a warm heart.

"The words of wise men are heard in quiet" (Eccles. ix. 17). Let the reproof be as sharp as thou wilt; but the spirit must be meek. *Passion* raiseth the blood of him that is reproved; but *compassion* turns his bowels. We must not denounce wrath in wrath.

Preach diligently. All the water is lost that runs beside the mill, and all thy thoughts are waste which help thee not to do God's work withal in thy general or particular calling. The bee will not sit on a flower

SERVANTS AND SERVICE

where no honey can be sucked, neither should the Christian. Why sittest thou here idle? thou shouldst say to thy soul, when thou hast so much to do for God and thy soul, and so little time to despatch it in?

X

READING AND MEDITATION

"Give attendance to reading, to exhortation, to doctrine. . . . Meditate upon these things."
1 TIMOTHY iv. 13–15.

MEDITATION is to the sermon what the harrow is to the seed, it covers those truths which else might have been picked or washed away.

An affectionate hearer will not be a forgetful hearer. Love helps the memory: Can a woman forget her child, or a maid her ornaments, or a bride her attire? No, they love them too well; were the truths of God thus precious to thee, thou wouldst with David think of them day and night. Even when the Christian, through weakness of memory, cannot remember the very words he hears, to repeat them; yea, then he keeps the power and savour of them in his spirit, as when sugar is dissolved in wine you cannot see it, but you may taste it; when meat is eaten and digested, it is not to be found as it was received, but the man is cheered and strengthened by it, more able to walk and work than before, by which you may know it is not lost: so you may taste the truths the Christian heard, in his spirit, see them in his life.

Till the heart be touched the mind will not be fixed. Therefore you may observe, it is said, God opened the heart of Lydia "that she attended" (Acts xvi. 14). The mind goes of the will's errand; we spend our thoughts on what our hearts propose. If the heart hath no sense of its ignorance, or no desires after God, no wonder such a one listens not what the preacher saith, his heart sends his mind another way. "They sit before thee as my people," saith God, "but their heart goeth after their covetousness."

When the soul stands upon this Pisgah of meditation, looking by an eye of faith, upon all the great and precious things laid up by a faithful God for him, it is easy to despise the world's love and wrath ; but, alas ! it is hard for us to go up thither who are so short-breathed, and soon tired with a few steps up this mount of God. Would we but frequently retire from the world, and bestow some of that time in secret waiting upon God, which we lavish out upon inferior pleasures, and entertainments of the creature, we should invite God's Holy Spirit to us. Let a wicked man set up a lust for his thoughts to dally with, and the devil will soon be at his elbow to assist him. And shall we not believe the Holy Spirit as ready to lend His helping hand to a holy meditation ? Doubtless He is. Spread thou thy sails and the Spirit will fill them with His heavenly breath. Be thou but careful to provide fuel, gather matter for meditation, set thy thoughts at work upon it, and the Spirit of God will kindle thy affections. " While I was musing," saith David, " the fire burned " (Ps. xxxix. 3).

Meditation fills the heart with heavenly matter, but prayer gives the discharge and pours it forth upon God. . . . Meditation is prayer's handmaid, to wait on it before and after the performance. It is as the plough before the sower, to prepare the heart for the duty of prayer, and as the harrow to cover the seed when it is sown.

Deadness in the heart of a saint will damp his zeal, if not cleared by daily watchfulness. Look, therefore, narrowly whence thy cooling comes; perhaps thy heart is too much let out upon the world in the day, and at night thy spirits are spent, when thou shouldst be in prayer. If thou wilt be hotter in duty, thou must be colder towards the world. Now, there is no better way for this, than to set thy soul under the frequent meditation of Christ's love to thee, thy relation to Him, with the great and glorious things thou expectest from Him; but if you let your heart continue soaking in the thoughts of an inordinate love to the world, you will find when you come to pray, that your hearts will be as a wet log at the back of a fire, long in kindling, and soon out again. Perhaps the deadness of thy heart in prayer ariseth from not having a deep sense of thy wants, and the mercies thou art in need of. Couldst thou but pray feelingly, thou wouldst pray fervently. The hungry man needs no help to teach him how to beg.

Prize the word, feed on the word, whether it be in public, or in a conference with some Christian friend, or in secret reading and meditation by thy solitary self. Let none of these be disused, or carnally used by thee. When thy stomach fails *to* the word, thy faith must needs begin to fail *on* the word.

But you will say, If we had so much time to spare as others, we would not be so unacquainted with the Scriptures. Could God find heart and time to pen and send this love-letter to thee, and thou find none to read and peruse it! The sick man no time to look on his physician's prescription!

The condemned malefactor to look on his prince's letter of grace, wherein a pardon is signed! Must the world have all thy time and swallow thee up alive! Art thou such a slave to thy pelf, as to tie thy soul to thy purse strings; and take no more time for the saving of it, than this cruel master will afford thee! Who gave thee leave thus to overlade thyself with the incumbrance of the world? Is not God the Lord of thy time? Why did you not read My word, and meditate thereon? will Christ say at that day. Darest thou, then, be so impudent as to say, Lord, I was overcharged with the cares, and drunk with the love of the world, and, therefore, I could not! Well, if this be the thief that robs thee of thy *time*, get out of his hands, lest it also rob thee of thy *soul*. What calling more encumbering than a soldier's, and of all the soldiers, the general's? Such an one was Joshua, yet he had a strict command given him to study the Scriptures: (Josh. i. 8) "This book shall not depart out of thy mouth; but thou shalt meditate therein day and night." Must Joshua, in the midst of drums and trumpets, and distractions of war, find time to meditate on the law of God, and shall a few trivial occasions in thy private calling discharge thee from the same duty?

Take heed thou comest not to the Scriptures with an unholy heart. If ever you know the mind of God in His word, the Spirit must impart it to you. And will He that is so holy take thee by thy foul hand, to lead thee into truth? No, thy doom is set, "None of the wicked shall understand" (Dan. xii. 10). If we have the truth for our guest, and be acquainted with the mind and will of God, we must have a holy heart for its lodging!

Go to God by prayer for a key to unlock the mysteries of His word. It is not the plodding but the praying soul, that will get this treasure of scripture knowledge. God often brings a truth to the Christian's hand as a return of prayer, which he had long hunted for in vain with much labour and study: "There is a God in heaven that revealeth secrets" (Dan. ii. 28); and where doth He reveal the secrets of His word but at the throne of grace? "From the first day," saith the angel, "that thou didst set thine heart to understand, and to chasten thyself before thy God, thy words were heard, and I am come for thy words"; that is for thy prayer (Dan. x. 12). And what was this heavenly messenger's errand to Daniel but to open more fully the Scripture to him? as appears by verse 14 compared with verse 21. This holy man had got some knowledge by his study in the word, and this sets him a-praying, and prayer fetched an angel from heaven to give him more light.

"Thy word have I hid in mine heart, that I might not sin against thee" (Ps. cxix. 11). It was not the Bible in his hand to read it, not the word on his tongue to speak of it; but the hiding it in his heart, that he found effectual against sin.

"Quench not the Spirit, despise not prophesyings" (1 Thess. v. 19, 20). They are coupled together; he that despiseth one loseth both. If the scholar be too proud to learn of the usher, he is unworthy to be taught by the master.

"They shall turn away their ears from the truth, and shall be turned unto fables" (2 Tim. iv. 3, 4). Satan commonly stops the ear from hearing sound doctrine, before he opens it to embrace corrupt.

XI

PRAYER AND THANKSGIVING

"Be careful for nothing; but in everything by prayer and supplication with thanksgiving let your requests be made known unto God."

PHILIPPIANS iv. 6.

*P*RAYER *the sign of life.* What is prayer, but the breathing forth of that grace which is breathed into the soul by the Holy Spirit? When God breathed into man the breath of life, he became a living soul; so when God breathes into the creature the breath of spiritual life, he becomes a praying soul: "Behold, he prayeth," saith God of Paul to Ananias (Acts ix. 11). Praying is the same to the new creature, as crying to the natural. The child is not learned by art to cry, but by nature—it comes into the world crying. Praying is not a lesson got by forms and rules of art, but flowing from principles of new life.

Prayer and reality. Prayer is an act in which we have immediately to do with the great God, to whom we approach in prayer. It is too sacred a duty to be performed between sleeping and waking, with a heavy eye or a drowsy heart; this God complained of: "There is none that calleth upon Thy name, that stirreth up himself to take hold of Thee" (Isa. lxiv. 7). He counts it no prayer where the heart is not stirred up and awake. Our behaviour in prayer hath an universal influence upon all the passages of our whole life; as a man is in prayer, so he is likely to be in all the rest; if he is careless in praying, then he is negligent in hearing and loose in his walking. Prayer is the channel, in which the stream of divine grace, blessing, and comfort, runs from God into the heart; dam up the channel and the stream is stopped.

Prayer and integrity. "If I regard iniquity in my heart, the Lord will not hear me" (Ps. lxvi. 18). Now, when God refuseth to hear, we may be sure the Spirit

PRAYER AND THANKSGIVING

refuseth to assist; for God never rejects a prayer which His Spirit indites. Hast thou defiled thyself with any known sin? Think not to have Him help thee in *prayer*, till He hath helped thee to *repent*; He will carry thee to the *laver* before He goes with thee to the *altar*.

Take heed thou prayest not with a reservation : be sure thou renouncest what thou wouldst have God remit. . . . He that desires not to be purged from the filth of sin, prays in vain to be eased of the guilt. If we love the work of sin, we must take the wages. A false heart could be willing to have his sin covered, but the sincere desires his heart may be cleansed. David begged a clean heart as well as a quiet conscience : " Blot out all mine iniquities ; create in me a clean heart, O God " (Ps. li. 9, 10). In nothing do our hearts more cheat us than in our prayers, and in no requests more than those which are levelled against our lusts. That is oftentimes *least intended*, which is *most pretended*. . . . The saint's prayer may miscarry from some secret grudge that is lodged in his heart against his brother.

Prayer and diligence. God hath appointed prayer as a help to our diligence, not as a cloak for our sloth. Idle beggars are welcome neither to God's door nor man's. What! wilt thou lift up thy hands to God in prayer, and then put them in thy pocket? Is it a lust thou art praying against? And dost thou sit down idle to see whether it will now die alone? Will that prayer slay one lust, that lets another (thy sloth I mean) live under its nose? Dost thou think to walk loosely all day, yielding thyself, and betraying the glory of God into the hands of thy lust, and then mend all with a prayer at night?

O Christian, should it not make thee blush much more, to see the whole town up, and as busy as bees in a garden, one flying this way, and another that way, and all to bring a little more of this world's perishing pelf into their hive, out of which, death ere long

PRAYER AND THANKSGIVING

will drive them, and force them to leave what with so much pains they have gathered for others; while thou sleepest away thy precious time, though thou art sure to carry thy gettings into the other world with thee, and there enjoy the fruit of thy short labour here, with everlasting glory!

Prayer and watching. He that prays and watcheth not, is like him that sows a field with precious seed, but leaves the gate open for hogs to come and rout it up. . . . "Watch and pray," saith Christ to His disciples; He knew they could not do that work sleeping. But it is not enough to keep the eye awake, if thou sufferest it to wander: "Turn away mine eyes from beholding vanity; and quicken thou me in thy way" (Ps. cxix. 37). To pray, and not watch what becomes of our prayer is a great folly, and no little sin. What is this but to take the name of God in vain? Yet thus do many knock at God's door, and then run away to the world and think no more of their prayers.

Prayer and perseverance. By "praying always" we are exhorted to the daily, constant exercise of prayer; by "praying with perseverance," we are pressed to bear up against discouragements, as to any particular request we may make at the throne of grace, and not to give over, though we have not a speedy answer to it; so that the former is opposed to a neglect of the duty in its stated seasons, and the latter to a fainting in our spirits, as to any particular suit we put up.

Prayer and supplication. "Praying . . . with all perseverance and *supplication* for all saints." In praying for saints you must pray for all: I do not mean for quick and dead; prayer is a means to wait upon them in their way; at death, when they are at their journey's end, prayers are useless, and the wicked in that estate are beneath, the saints above, our prayers; we cannot help the wicked, the tree is fallen, and so it must lie. We read of a change the body shall have after death. Vile bodies may, but filthy souls cannot after death be made glorious:

if they leave the body filthy, so shall they meet it at the resurrection. As the wicked are beyond our help, so the saints are above all need of our help. . . . We are to love all saints, therefore to pray for all. The new creature never wants its new nature; if God loves all His children, then wilt thou all thy brethren, or not one of them. When Paul commends Christians for this grace of love, he doth it thus: (Eph. i. 15) "After I heard of your faith in the Lord Jesus, and love unto all the saints." Now, if we love all, we cannot but pray for all.

Though we are to pray for all saints, yet some call for a more special remembrance at our hands: for instance, those that are near to us by bond of nature as well as of grace. "A brother beloved, specially to me, but how much more unto thee, both in the flesh, and in the Lord" (Philemon 16). You are to pray particularly for those that are in distress: whoever you forget, remember these: this is a fit season for love. A friend for adversity is as proper as fire for a winter's day : Job's friends chose the right time to visit him, but took not the right course of improving their visit : had they spent the time in praying for him which they did in hot disputes with him, they had profited him, and pleased God more.

Prayer and thanksgiving. Prayer is a means to dispose the heart to praise. When David begins a psalm with prayer, he commonly ends it with praise. That Spirit which leads a soul out of itself to God for supply, will direct it to the same God with His praise. We do not borrow money of one man and return it to another. If God hath been thy strength, surely thou wilt make Him thy song. The thief comes not to thank a man for what he steals out of his yard. Mercies ill got are commonly as ill spent, because they are not sanctified, and so become fuel to feed lusts.

As a necessary ingredient in all our prayers : Let your requests be made known with *thanksgiving* (Phil. iv. 6). This spice must be in all our offerings. He that prays for a mercy he wants, and is not thankful for mercies received, may seem mindful of himself, but is forgetful of God, and so takes the right course to shut his prayers out of doors. God will not put His mercies into a rent purse; and such is an unthankful heart.

Daniel, when in the very shadow of death, the plot being laid to take away his life, prayed three times a day, and gave thanks before his God (Dan. vi. 10). To have heard him pray in that great strait would not have afforded so much matter for wonder; but to have his heart in tune for giving thanks in such a sad hour was admirable.

Prayer and trial. When prayer cannot prevail to keep a temporal mercy alive, yet it will have a powerful influence to keep thy heart alive when that dies. O, it is sad, when a man's estate and comfort are buried in the same grave together. None will bear the loss of an enjoyment so patiently, as he that was exercised in prayer while he had it. The more David prayed for his child while alive, the fewer tears he shed for it when dead.

Prayer and prosperity. Prayer is not a winter garment : it is then to be worn indeed, but not to be left off in the summer of prosperity. If you would find some at prayer, you must stay till it thunders and lightens ; and not go to them except it be in a storm. Pray in prosperity, that thou mayest speed when thou prayest in adversity ; own God now, that He may acknowledge thee then. Shall that friend be welcome to us, who never gives us a visit but when he comes to borrow ? Pray in prosperity, that thou mayest not be ensnared by it. Prosperity is no friend to the memory, therefore we are cautioned so much to beware when we are full, lest we forget God. You shall find, in Scripture, that the saints have had their saddest falls on the most even ground. Noah, who had seen the whole world drowned in water, no sooner was safe on shore, but himself is drowned in wine,

David's heart was fixed when in the wilderness, but his wanton eye rolled and wandered when he walked upon the terrace of his palace.

Morning and evening prayer. Prayer must be the key of the morning, and lock of the night. We show not ourselves Christians, if we do not open our eyes with prayer when we rise, and shut them again with the same key we lie down at night. Pray as often as you please besides.

If you will have fire for your evening sacrifice, labour to keep what is already on thy altar from going out. What you fill the vessel with you must expect to draw thence: if water be put in, we cannot, without a miracle, think to draw wine. What! art thou all day filling thy heart with earth (God being not in all thy thoughts), and dost thou look to draw heaven thence at night? He that is heavenly in his earthly employments, will be the less worldly in his heavenly. It was a sweet speech of a dying saint, that he was going to change his place but not his company.

Broken prayer. Sometimes thou hearest one pray with a moving expression, whilst thou canst hardly get out a few broken words in duty, and thou art ready to accuse thyself and to admire him; as if the gilt of the key made it open the door better. "Elijah was a man subject to like passions as we are, and he prayed" (James v. 17). A weak hand with a sincere heart is able to turn the key in prayer.

Ejaculatory prayer. Ejaculatory prayer to God, is the short dagger thou art to use for thy defence against temptation, when thou hast no time to draw the long sword of solemn prayer. Thus thou mayest pray in any place, company, or employment.

Public prayer. When thou prayest before others, observe on what thou bestowest thy chief care and zeal, whether on the externals or internals of prayer; that which is exposed to the eye and ear of men, or that for the eye and ear of God; the devout posture of thy body, or the inward devotion of thy soul; the pomp of thy words, or the power of thy faith; the agitation of thy bodily spirits in the vehemency of thy voice, or the fervency of thy spirit in heart-breaking affections. These inward workings are the very soul of prayer. The sincere soul dares not be rude in his outward posture; he is careful of his words, that they may be grave and pertinent, neither would he pray them asleep who join with him, by a cold manner of delivering his prayer; but still it is the inward disposition of his heart he principally looks to, knowing well, that it is possible to warm in prayer, thereby benefiting others, and at the same time have his own heart cold and idle; therefore he doth not count he prays well, except he finds his own affections drawn out. The hypocrite, if he comes off the duty with the applause of others in the external performance, is well pleased.

Formal prayer. Take heed of formal praying, this is as baneful to grace as not praying. A plaster, though proper, and of sovereign virtue, yet if it be laid on cold, may do more hurt than good.

Dost thou think that God will welcome that prayer to heaven which hath not thy heart to bear it company? And how can thy heart go with it, when thou hast sent it another way? Will God hear thee when thou mockest Him? And if this be not to mock Him, what is? Like children that give a knock at a door, and then run away to their play again; thus thou raisest thy voice to God, and then are gone in thy roving thought to hold converse with the world, or worse. Is not this trifling with God? Satan disturbs thee *in* praying, that he may make thee weary *of* praying. Indeed he is not likely to miss his mark, if thou lettest these vermin go on to breed in thy heart; for these will rob thee of the sweetness of prayer; and when the *marrow* is once out, thou wilt easily be persuaded to throw the *bone* away.

He is in danger to forsake his meat, who hath lost his relish for it. Prayer is a tedious work for him who hath no pleasure in it : and weariness in it stands next door to weariness of it.

The best way to keep vessels from leaking is to let them stand full. A vain heart *out* of prayer, will be little better *in* prayer. Walk in the company of sinful thoughts all the day, and thou wilt hardly shut the door upon them, when thou goest into thy closet. Thou hast taught them to be bold ; they will now plead acquaintance with thee, and crowd in after thee, like little children, who if you play with them, will cry after you when you would be rid of their company.

Beware that thy constant daily prayer doth not degenerate into a lifeless formality. What we do commonly we are prone to do slightly. He is a rare Christian that keeps his course in prayer, and yet grows not to pray of mere course. He that watcheth his heart all day, is most likely to find it in tune for prayer at night; whereas loose walking breeds lazy praying.

Never was any formal prayer of the Holy Spirit's making; when He comes it is a time of life.

Lengthy prayer. Pray often rather than very long. It is difficult to remain long in prayer, and not slacken in our affections. Especially observe this in social prayers; for when we pray in company, we must consider them that travel with us: as Jacob said: "I will lead on softly, as the children are able to endure."

Hindrances to prayer. There is an antipathy between sinning and praying. The child that hath misspent the day in play abroad, steals to bed at night, for fear of a chiding from his father. Sin and prayer are such contraries, that it is impossible at one stride to step from one to another.

Another method Satan hath to make the Christian put off prayer is some worldly business that is to be dispatched. Take heed of overcharging thyself with worldly business, which is done when thou graspest more thereof than will consist with thy Christian calling. God allows thee to give to the world that which is the world's, but He will not suffer thee to pay the world that which is due to Him. We could not easily want time to pray, if our hearts would but persuade our heads to devise and study how our other affairs might be disposed of without prejudice to our devotions. That cloth which a bungler thinks too little for a garment, a good workman can make one of it, and leave some for another use also. O, there is a great deal of art in cutting out time with little loss. Some look upon every minute of time spent in the closet, as lost in the shop. Does the husbandman mow the less for whetting his scythe? Doth a good grace before meat spoil the dinner? No. nor doth prayer hinder the Christian either in his employments or enjoyments, but expedites the one, and sanctifies the other. "Acknowledge God in all thy ways, and lean not to thy own understanding."

Godliness hath the "promise of the life that now is, and of that which is to come" (1 Tim. iv. 8). This earth below, to a saint, is a land of promise, though not the land that is chiefly promised. God hath not promised him heaven, and left him to the wide world to shift for his outward subsistence; He hath not bid them live by faith, for their souls, and live by their wits, for their bodies. No; He that hath promised to give him "grace and glory," hath also said, "No good thing will He withhold from them that walk uprightly" (Ps. lxxxiv. 11). Their bill of fare here is provided as well as their inheritance hereafter.

Neglect of prayer. When Saul had given over inquiring after God, we hear him knocking at the devil's door, and asking counsel of a witch. Take heed of living near the tempter! If Satan might have his wish, surely it would be this, that the creature might live prayerless.

Satan cannot but deny but great wonders have been wrought by prayer. As the spirit of prayer goes up, so his kingdom goes down. Satan's stratagems against prayer are three. First, If he can, he will keep thee from prayer. If that be not feasible, secondly, he will strive to interrupt thee in prayer. And, thirdly, if that plot takes not, he will labour to hinder the success of thy prayer.

"Thou castest off fear, and restrainest prayer before God" (Job xv. 4). Eliphaz's doctrine was true, though his application was false. Sins of commission are the usual punishments that God inflicts on persons for sins of omission: he that leaves a duty, may fear to be left to commit a crime: he that turns his ear from the truth, takes the ready course to be given over to believe fables (2 Tim. iv. 4): he that casteth off prayer, it is a wonder if you find him not, ere long, cast into some foul sin.

Answers to prayer. He hath engaged to answer the prayers of His people, and fulfil the desires of them that fear Him (Ps. cxlv. 19); but it proves a long voyage sometimes before the praying saint hath the return of his adventure. There comes often a long and sharp winter between the sowing time of prayer and the reaping. He hears us, indeed, as soon as we pray, but we often do not hear of Him so soon. Prayers are not long on their journey to heaven, but long coming thence in a full answer. Never was faithful prayer lost at sea. No merchant trades with such certainty as the praying saint. Some prayers, indeed, have a longer voyage than others, but then they come with the richer lading at last.

Sometimes we have speedy return of prayers—"In the day that I cried, thou answeredst me." While the church were at God's door praying for Peter's deliverance, Peter is knocking at theirs, to tell them their prayer is heard.

XII

PATIENCE AND HOPE

" Whatsoever things were written aforetime were written for our learning, that we through patience and comfort of the scriptures might have hope."
ROMANS xv. 4.

HOPE hath an eye that can see heaven in a cloudy day, and an anchor that can find firm land under a weight of waters to hold by ; it can expect good out of evil.

True hope is a jewel that no one wears but Christ's bride ; a grace with which no one is graced but the believer's soul. Christless and hopeless are joined together (Eph. ii. 12).

We are directed to " take the helmet of salvation " ; and this not for some particular occasion, and then hang it up till another extraordinary strait calls us to take it down, and use it again ; but we must take it so as never to lay it aside, till God shall take off this helmet, to put on a crown of glory in the room of it. " Be sober, and hope to the end," is the apostle Peter's counsel (1 Peter i. 13).

The hope of heaven leaves a blot upon the world in the Christian's thoughts. He that looks on heaven, must needs look off earth. The soul's eye can as little as the body's be above and below at the same time. Here is not my hope, saith the soul, and therefore not my haunt : my hope is in heaven, from whence I look for my Saviour, and my salvation to come with Him.

Hast thou heaven *in hope?* It is more than if thou hadst the whole world *in hand.* The greatest monarch the earth hath will be glad, in a dying hour, to change his crown for thy helmet ; his crown will not procure him this helmet, but thy helmet will bring thee to a crown ; a crown not of gold, but of glory, which, once on, shall never be taken off.

Why are men dull and heavy in the service of God? Truly because their hopes are so. Hopeless and lifeless go together. No wonder the work goes hardly off hand, when men have no hope to be well paid for their labour. He that thinks he works for a song, will not sing at his work—I mean forward it. The best customer is sure to be served best and first; and him we count the best customer whom we hope will be the best paymaster. If God be thought so, we will leave all to do His business. Nothing better to clear the soul of sloth and listlessness of spirit in the service of God than hope well improved and strengthened. It is the very physic which the apostles prescribe for this disease: "We desire that every one of you do shew the same diligence to the full assurance of hope unto the end: that ye be not slothful" (Heb. vi. 11, 12).

"What manner of persons ought ye to be in all holy conversation and godliness, looking for and hasting unto the coming of the day of God?" (2 Peter iii. 11, 12). Live up to thy hopes, Christian; let there be a decorum kept between thy principles and thy practices—thy hope of heaven, and walk on earth. The eye should direct the foot. Thou lookest for salvation; walk the same way thy eye looks. There is a decorum, which if a Christian doth not observe in his walking, he betrays his high calling and hopes unto scorn. To look high and live low, how ridiculous it appears!

Let thy hope of heaven moderate thy affections to earth. "Be sober, and hope," saith the apostle (1 Peter i. 13). You that look for so much in another world, may be very well content with a little in this. Nothing more unbecomes a heavenly hope than an earthly heart.

I doubt not but every gracious person finds the nearer to heaven he gets *in his hopes*, the farther he goes from earth *in his desires*. When he stands upon these battlements of heaven, he can look down upon this dunghill world as a little dust-heap, next to nothing.

Let thy hope of heaven conquer thy fear of death. Why shouldst thou be afraid to die, who hopest to live by dying? Is the apprentice afraid of the day when his time will be out?—he that runs a race, of coming too soon to his goal?—the pilot troubled when he sees his harbour? Death is all this to thee! Thy indenture expires, and thy jubilee is come; thy race is run, and the crown won, and is sure to drop on thy head when thy soul goes out of thy body. Thy voyage, how troublesome soever it was in its sailing, is now happily finished, and death doth but land thy soul on the shore of eternity at thy heavenly Father's door, never to be put to sea more.

The Turks say, they do not think we Christians believe heaven to be such a glorious place as we profess and talk of; for, if we did, we would not be so afraid to go thither. Christian, understand aright what message death brings to thee, and the fear of it will be over; it snatcheth thee, indeed, from this world's enjoyments, but it leads thee to the felicities of another, incomparably better. And who, at a feast, will chide the servant that takes away the first course to make room for the second to be set on, that consists of far greater delicacies!

A sad heart does not become a living hope. Christ takes no more delight to dwell in a sad heart, than we in a dark house; therefore, let in the light which sheds its beams upon thee from the promise, or else thy sweet Saviour will be gone. We do not entertain our friends in a dark room, or sit by those who visit us mopish, lest they should think we are weary of their company. Christ brings such good news with Him, as may bespeak better welcome with thee than a disconsolate spirit.

Wouldst thou not have thy hope strong? Then keep thy conscience pure. Thou canst not defile one, without weakening the other,

Living godly in this present world, and looking for the blessed hope laid up for us in the other, are both conjoined (Titus ii. 13). A soul wholly void of godliness, must needs be as destitute of all true hope; and the godly person that is loose and careless in his holy walking will soon find his hope languishing. All sin disposeth the soul that tampers with it, to trembling fears, and shakings of heart. God forbid, Christian, that death should find thee wanton and negligent in thy walking, that he should surprise thee lying in the puddle of some sin! Can a bird fly, when one of its wings is broken? Faith and a good conscience are hope's two wings; if, therefore, thou hast wounded thy conscience by any sin, renew thy repentance, that so thou mayest exercise faith for the pardon of it, and redeem thy hope, when the mortgage that is now upon it shall be taken off. If a Jew had pawned his bedclothes, God provided mercifully, that it should be restored before night; "For," saith he, "that is his covering; wherein shall he sleep?" (Exod. xxii. 27).

Truly, hope is the saint's covering, wherein he wraps himself, when he lays his body down to sleep in the grave: "My flesh," saith David, "shall rest in hope" (Ps. xvi. 9). A sad going to the bed of grave he hath, who hath no hope of a resurrection to life.

Hope is the handkerchief that God puts into His people's hands, to wipe the tears from their eyes, which their present troubles, and long stay of expected mercies, draw from them (Jer. xxxi. 16, 17): "Refrain thy voice from weeping, and thine eyes from tears: for thy work shall be rewarded, saith the Lord; and they shall come again from the land of the enemy. And there is hope in thine end."

"The Lord direct your hearts into the love of God, and into the patient waiting for Christ" (2 Thess. iii. 5). It is a way you will never find, a work you will never be able to do of yourselves thus to wait patiently till Christ come, "the Lord," therefore, "direct your hearts" into it. Love Him, and you will wait for Him. So Jude 21: "Keep yourselves in the love of God, looking for the mercy of our Lord Jesus Christ unto eternal life."

XIII

A BASKET OF FRAGMENTS

"The words of the wise are as goads."
ECCLESIASTES xii. 11.

THE believer is to persevere in his Christian course to the end of his life; his work and his life must go off the stage together.

The fearful are in the forlorn of those who march to hell (Rev. xxi. 8).

O how uncomely a sight is it, a bold sinner, and a fearful saint!

Christ never lost a battle even when He lost His life.

He that hath God's heart cannot want His arm.

This goodly fabric of heaven and earth hath not been built, but as a stage whereon God would in time act what He decreed in heaven of old.

One Almighty is more than many mighties. All these mighty sins and devils make not any almighty sin, or an almighty devil.

A proud heart and a lofty mountain are never fruitful.

"Pray." But how? "Without ceasing."
"Rejoice." But when? "Evermore."
"Give thanks." For what? "In everything."

God will not have His kingdom, either in the heart or in the world, maintained by carnal policy.

When afflicted, love can allow thee to groan, but not to grumble.

Mercy should make us ashamed, wrath afraid to sin.

Whoever thou art, thou art base-born till born again.

Christ and Satan divide the whole world; Christ will bear no equal, and Satan no superior, and therefore hold in with both thou canst not.

Sin only sets Satan in the throne.

Sinners dying in their sins, cannot hope to have a better resurrection than they have a death.

Since man was turned out of paradise, he can do nothing without labour, except sin.

We must either lay self aside, or God will lay us aside.

Bernard used to say, when he heard any scandalous sin of a professor, *Hodie illi, cras mihi.* He fell to-day, I may stumble to-morrow.

A soul in meditation is on his way to prayer.

It is impossible for a naughty heart to think well of an afflicting God.

The great talkers of religion are oft the least doers.

Does thy heavenly Father keep so starved a house that the devil's scraps will go down with thee?

No truth but has some error next door.

No action so little, but we may in it do God or the devil some service, and therefore none too little for our care to be bestowed on.

It is not enough to have truth on our side, if we have not truth in our hearts.

Hypocrisy is a lie with a fair cover over it.

None sooner topple over into error, than such who have a dishonest heart with a nimble head. The richest soil, without culture, is most tainted with weeds.

Thou must live by thy faith, not another's. Labour to see truth with thy own eyes.

He that maintains any error from the Bible, bears false witness against God.

He that abandons the truth of God, renounceth the God of truth.

Error is short lived; "a lying tongue is but for a moment"; but truth's age runs parallel with God's eternity.

It is no matter what is the sign, though an angel, that hangs without, if the devil and sin dwell within.

Heaven is worth the having, though thou goest poor and ragged, yea, naked, thither.

The gospel, what is it, but God's heart in print.

The Christian's love to Christ takes fire at Christ's love to him. No such picklock to open the heart as love.

You never knew a man full of self-confidence and self-abasement together. The conscience cannot abound with a sense of sin, and the heart with self-conceit at the same time.

A temptation comes very forcibly when it runs with the tide of our own wills.

"Seest thou a man wise in his own conceit? there is more hope of a fool than of him" (Prov. xxvi. 12); of all fools the conceited fool is the worst. Pride makes a man incapable of receiving counsel.

Exercise thy faith, if thou meanest to preserve thy faith. We live by faith, and faith lives by exercise,

The devil is wily, thou hadst need be wary.

None long for heaven more than those that enjoy most of heaven.

" Faithful are the wounds of a friend, but the kisses of an enemy are deceitful " (Prov. xxvii. 6). God's wounds cure ; sin's kisses kill.

Never think to find honey in the pot, when God writes poison on the cover.

Sin disturbs the inward peace of the soul and the outward peace of the world.

Thou knowest, sinner, already, the best of thy sinful pleasure, but not the worst of thy punishment.

If thou wilt play the mountebank, choose not the pulpit for thy stage.

The less conscience barks at present, the more it will bite when it shall be unmuzzled.

Either use the world as if thou usedst it not, or you will pray as if you prayed not.

The faster a man rides if he be in a wrong road, the farther he goes out of his way.

He that is impatient, and cannot wait on God for a mercy, will not easily submit to Him in a denial.

Man's words will not break thy bones.

Cease to pray and thou wilt begin to sin. Prayer is not only a means to prevail for mercy, but also to prevent sin.

Where God is on one side, you may be sure to find the devil on the other.

He that shows any kindness to a saint, is sure to have God for his paymaster.

The work of salvation cannot be done by the candle-light of a natural understanding, but by the sunlight of a gospel revelation.

God had Nero a closer prisoner than he had Paul.

Error is but a day younger than truth.

Christ passeth oft by palaces to visit the poor cottages. Pilate missed Christ on the bench, while the poor thief finds Him, and heaven with Him, on the cross.

Ignorance is the mother of persecution.

That book must be worth reading, that hath God for the author.

We must come to good works by faith, and not to faith by good works.

It was a charge long ago laid upon Christianity, that it was better known in leaves of books than in the lives of Christians.

It is better to die honourably than live shamefully.

It is easier to bow at the name, than to stoop to the cross of Jesus Christ.

The head may be ripe, and the heart rotten.

Prayer is a great heart-easer.

The sins of teachers are the teachers of sins.

PRINTED BY
WILLIAM BRENDON AND SON, LTD.
PLYMOUTH